Real Like the Daisies, or Real like I Love You?

Essays in radical Quakerism

David Boulton

Dales Historical Monographs
in association with
Quaker Universalist Group
2002

Published by
Dales Historical Monographs, Hobsons Farm, Dent, Cumbria,
England LA10 5RF
Tel: 015396 25321 ★ email publications@dentdale.com
in association with
Quaker Universalist Group, 7 Barewell Close,
St. Marychurch, Torquay, Devon TQ1 4PB

ISBN 0 9511578 5 X

Typesetting by Dales Historical Monographs
Printed by
Stramongate Press, Aynam Mills, Little Aynam, Kendal,
Cumbria LA9 7AH

Contents

Introduction

Nearly all the essays, papers and short pieces in this collection have been published before in various periodicals - *Friends Quarterly, The Friend, Proceedings of the Quaker Theology Seminar, Political Theology, Sea of Faith* and *New Humanist*. I therefore owe the reader an explanation as to why I have brought them together under one set of covers.

There is, first, a practical reason. Either because they have seen a reference to one of the papers in someone else's work, or because they have heard of it in other ways and want to follow something up, Friends write from time to time asking for copies or details of publication. Not infrequently, they then ask for details of other articles in similar vein. I hope that I'll be spared time at the photo-copier by this exercise in vanity publishing, supported as it is by the Quaker Universalist Group!

But there is another reason. Although written over a six year period, for different publications and (in the case of the *Sea of Faith* pieces) for a wider readership than the Society of Friends, these essays broadly hang together as my contribution to radical new thinking in the Society and the wider family of churches and faith communities. That we need radical new thinking is, I hope, obvious: we are twenty-first century people increasingly ill at ease with language and thought forms rooted in the seventeenth century and earlier. I do not for a moment imagine or claim that my contribution to new thinking is either the only or the most important one in the field: of course not. But it is a contribution, and I hope that, seen as a developing body of work rather than as isolated products of my gadfly mentality, it will take its modest place among the weightier contributions of fully-fledged Quakers and full-time theologians.

At the heart of what I am saying in the theological essays in Part 1 is that our old ways of envisioning God no longer do the business in our contemporary world. I am clear about that - but, readers may reasonably think, less clear about what we do about it. Do we, as Gerrard Winstanley did three and a half centuries ago, drop "God" altogether as a stumbling-block and a confusion, a concept so thoroughly worn and torn by theological wrangling that it has become a drag rather than a spur to the more abundant life we seek? Or do we breathe new life into it, discarding the supernaturalism in which it was so long enveloped, and finding a fresh use for it as the supercharged symbol of our most precious human values? Readers will detect first the one, then the other emphasis in the pieces that follow: the value of God-language affirmed more confidently in the title essay, *Real Like the Daisies, or Real Like I love You?*, than in, for instance, the later essay *What on Earth is Religious Humanism?*

The division of essays into theological, historical and reviews is somewhat arbitrary in that some of the theological essays (particularly *The Diversity of Truth* and *Jesus: History, Mystery or Story*) are necessarily historical, while the essays in Quaker history (particularly that on Winstanley) clearly have a thoroughly theological context. A few short reviews are included because they hopefully help flesh out the ideas discussed in the longer pieces. There is some repetition, particularly of favourite bytes of Blake and Arnold!

I have indulged in a certain amount of rewriting, either to improve on the originals or to remove or minimise references which might have been pertinent to the original readership but are likely to be lost in this new context. In particular, the Winstanley essay has been reconstructed from three different but overlapping articles and papers. Each piece is prefaced by a short explanatory note. Except in the title essay, I have not included the source notes which went with the original publications.

I am very much in the debt of the editors of the journals in which these pieces first appeared. Greater still, however, is my debt to fellow members of the Woodbrooke Quaker Theology Seminar, inspiringly led by Rex Ambler and Chas Raw. Seminar members subjected the title essay and the other QTS papers to their stringent criticism and review (though the final versions are of course my responsibility alone). I hope something in these papers will stimulate readers to study the published *Proceedings* of the Seminar (available from the Quaker Book Shop, Euston Road, London), in which will be found a number of perspectives very different from my own.

I owe a debt of gratitude, too, to my fellow-travellers in the Quaker Universalist Group, particularly to its chief energiser and motivator, Alec Davison. By no means all Quaker Universalists are 'Quaker Humanists', and I have greatly valued the critical perspectives of those Friends who share my coolness towards conservative Quakerism (with its aversion to theological thinking, and sometimes to thinking of any kind) but cannot join me in 'taking leave of God for God's sake'. Finally, I am no less grateful to fellow voyagers on the Sea of Faith, only a few of whom are Friends, who had less trouble with 'taking leave of God' but had to wait ten years before they could take leave of me as editor of their magazine in January 2002.

Nothing written here will stand the test of time. We are all renewed, and our ideas, speculations and convictions change as we hopefully grow in knowledge, wisdom, and even grace. In ten, perhaps in five years time, much of what I have written here will be cruelly exposed as time- and culture-limited, an expression of a mode of seeking particular to the turn of the twenty-first century. But I am confident that a core-meaning will survive, as it has already survived two centuries since William Blake reminded us that 'all deities reside in the human breast' and that 'mercy, pity, peace and love' is both God and 'the human form divine'. If we could grasp that, whether as Friends or as a much more inclusive fellowship of wholly human spirits, we would discover that we once again have a message for the world.

David Boulton
Hobsons Farm, Dent, Cumbria LA10 5RF
publications@dentdale.com

February 2002

Part One

God

Real Like the Daisies, or
Real Like I Love You?

This paper was prepared for the Woodbrooke Quaker Theology Seminar meetings in 1998/9 and, after constructive criticism and revision, was published in the QTS 'Proceedings' for 1999.

The title refers to a question said to have been asked by a child of her Quaker parents: is God "real", as things like daisies and elephants and mountains are real, or real like love, justice, beauty and truth? What do we mean when we describe God as real or nonreal?

"Forget the universalist/Christocentric debate, that's not where we are. Where we are ... is whether we can have a relationship with God or whether God is a personification, a metaphor for our highest ideals. That is the theological dilemma facing the Society at the moment." - *Harvey Gillman, Friends' Quarterly, April 1996.*

"How does it matter, or does it matter, if there are Friends who do not subscribe to the uniqueness of Jesus, or indeed to the realist idea of God? It seem(s) to me that this last topic held within itself the whole crux of what the Seminar was about." - *Michael Mitlehner, "Truth and Diversity: Proceedings of the Quaker Theology Seminar 1994/5".*

These two quotations, Harvey Gillman's from the Quaker mainstream and the late Michael Mitlehner's from the Quaker Theology Seminar, both urge an overriding importance for the question of what Friends in particular and religious communities in general mean today, at the end of the second "Christian" millenium, by the *reality* and *otherness* of "God". I want to agree with them about the *importance* of the question. But I want to challenge what I take to be the implication of at least the first, that God is *either* objectively "real" *or* not "real" at all. And I want to challenge the further implication that the spiritual health of the Society, as of the church at large, depends on its finding and affirming the "right" answer. This last implication is most clearly stated in Harvey Gillman's text, where he goes on to say:

"What we offer is the place and the support of a direct, spontaneous, individual and corporate relationship with the divine. If there is no relationship there is no Religious Society of Friends. If we cannot have a relationship with the divine, *if there is nothing there*, then I cannot see that any reference to our grand tradition of three hundred and fifty years... is at all relevant today" (my emphasis) [1].

Thus, in Harvey's view, at least as expressed here, the alternative to belief in an objectively real God is the belief that "there is nothing there", and the consequence of believing there is nothing there would be that Quaker tradition is empty and meaningless.

I want to argue, on the contrary, that the view Harvey is questioning, the view somewhat confusingly described since the late 1970s as "nonrealism", far from *denying* any reality to what we call the experience of God, actually *affirms* and cherishes the experience, defending it against a shallow reductionist materialism on the one front and the perils of an outmoded supernaturalism on the other. I want to suggest that those of us who have found "nonrealism" a valuable tool in the great work of making sense of things do *not* say "there is nothing there", even if we *do* find the notion of an "objectively real" God - person, spiritual entity, creative energy or whatever - unhelpful and irrelevant to our experience in postmodernity. So I want to explore in what sense "God" *is* real to the "nonrealist", and I want to argue that the sense in which "God" is "real" is not a *diminished* but a greatly *enhanced* sense. Not "God is *only* real in this *limited* sense," but "the experience of what we have traditionally called God is *no less* real than the most intense experience we can hope to have". And I want to position this kind of affirmative nonrealism within the historical Quaker tradition, in opposition to the misconception (as it seems to me) that it represents some deviant form, some faddish "notion" which, in so far as it has taken hold, is just the latest symptom of the way in which God's faithful Quakers have deserted Truth as they grope their way amid the encircling gloom of our wayward and godless age.

I take my title from a story told by Janet Scott of a little girl who asked if God was real. "Yes", she was assured, "God is real", to which she responded, "But is he real like the daisies or real like I love you?" This reminded me of my own daughter coming home from primary school, where she was taught by an evangelical teacher called Mr Dolan, and asking us whether God was true or just a story. We said he was a story, but a *true* story. This wasn't good enough for Katy, who pressed on: "But is God true like Mr Dolan says or true like you say?"

Philosophers would probably tell our wisely childish questioners that the distinction between the daisies and "I love you" doesn't run very deep. The traditional Platonist says both are *real*: biologists investigate the molecular structure of daisies and psychologists the neural mechanisms of love. They are both dealing with something real. The postmodernist or nonrealist also says daisies and "I love you" are in the same boat, in that both are *nonreal*: neither has any intrinsic meaning of its own, both are known to us as wholly human perceptions, where thing, word and consciousness of the thing and the word form an inseparable unity. Thus the distinction between the reality of the daisy and the reality of "I love you" is itself unreal. Nonrealism dissolves the old distinctions between a "straightforward" "common sense" kind of real and a non-material all-in-the-mind kind of real, suggesting that it may not always be helpful to talk of a "see, hear, smell, touch, taste" kind of representational reality. Daisy and love share a common reality as language symbols. They are both made manifest all in the mind, since the only world we can know is "all in the mind".

But our six-year-olds are not doing a philosophy class. There is, for them, *some* kind of distinction between the daisy which they *see* to be real and the "I love you" which they *feel* to be real. And they want to know, is God real like daisies and mummies and daddies and teachers, or real like love, beauty, jealousy, fear. The reality of a daisy, I understand them (and perhaps Harvey) to be saying, is that you can mow it, pluck it, make chains out of it, stick it in a pot on the mantlepiece, talk to it (if you are a Prince of Wales) or present it to your beloved. You can't do any of these things (except the last) with "I love you". Moreover, Harvey would seem to say if you can't mow it, pluck it, talk to it, "there's nothing there". Either it is real or it is an illusion. If it is real we are in business as a Society. If it is an illusion, we are a suitable case for treatment.

Nonrealists say reality is more complex and multi-layered than that. Not just the postmodernist philosophers but writers, poets, artists know this. Novelist and essayist Jeanette Winterson (*Oranges Are Not the Only Fruit*) offers a good definition of postmodern reality. It is "continuous, multiple, simultaneous, complex, abundant and partly invisible" [2]. That beautifully describes the reality of "I love you". It is also a pretty good description of the reality of God. And it is the question "In what sense is the experience of God real?" that theology addresses. To retreat from the language of realism and nonrealism to the more familiar categories of objective and subjective reality, is God best thought of as having the kind of objectivity our six-year-olds would assign to the daisies or the subjectivity of "I love you"?

There is a long historical tradition which has located "God" or "the divine" *within* rather than *beyond* humanity: the tradition of radical immanentism, in which early Quakerism was born. This tradition played down, if it did not altogether deny, the remoteness and "transcendence" of God, and played up the notion of God-within-humanity. Early Friends were accused of atheism for so emphasising the God within - the "inward light", "that of God in everyone" - that they seemed to orthodox churchpeople to deny the Almighty transcendent God altogether.

Some radicals on the Reformation Left *did* insist that God was wholly-within, subjective rather than objective, including some who were ridiculed for "ranting" and some who were mocked for "quaking". As post-Restoration Quakers slowly relapsed into respectable nonconformity, discarding much of their former theological radicalism, the torch of radical immanentism was picked up, first in the eighteenth century by other antinomian groups, and then in the nineteenth by radical Lutherans and the liberal fringes of orthodoxy. Thus William Blake (whose possible Muggletonian background has been suggested by E P Thompson [3]) emerges in the 1790s as the poet laureate of a passionate lyrical religious humanism, demonising Newton's scientifically real and reasonable God as a tyrannical and ridiculous Nobodaddy (rather as Gerrard Winstanley had described a real God as the very devil). Blake's God - since "all Deities reside in the Human breast" - is the imagined personification of the divinely-human values of mercy, pity, peace and love. (Does anyone today find Blake's God less real then Newton's?).

Blake's inspired poetry/theology is followed by the academic prose/theology of the German Lutherans D. F. Strauss (*The Life of Jesus Critically Examined*, 1835) and Ludwig Feuerbach, who argued in *The Essence of Christianity* (1841) that God had no independent, objective or "real" existence but was "the outward projection of man's inner nature". Feuerbach wrote, in George Eliot's translation, as any early Friend might have written: "The relations of child and parent, of husband and wife, of brother and friend - in general, of man to man - in short, all the moral relations, are *per se* religious. Life as a whole is, in its essential, substantial relations, throughout of a divine nature". A few years earlier (1817) John Keats had put it more passionately: "I am certain of nothing but of the holiness of the heart's affections", adding "and the truth of the imagination - what the imagination seizes as beauty must be truth - whether it existed before or not" [4].

Nor were the seventeenth-century radicals or Blake or Keats or Feuerbach saying anything completely new. Sixth-century Pseudo-Denis the Areopagite had insisted that God is "not one of the things that are". God is "Nothing": no thing. God does not exist. Indeed, Denis preferred (like Winstanley and Blake) not to use the word "God" at all - or, when he did, to couple it with "not-God" [5].

If this immanentist tradition, this assertion of God as not-a-thing-like-the-daisies, eventually ran out into modern secular humanism, this was perhaps because orthodox theology (which by the mid-1800s had gathered mainstream Quakerism into its evangelical fold) again reached for its biggest guns, the damning labels of "Blasphemy!" and "Atheism!", to drive it off religion's territory and into the arms of "free thought". There is a school of Anglican theology today which argues that by their uncompromising resistance to this resurgent Christian humanism the nineteenth century churches condemned themselves to be swept to the sidelines as the insights of Feuerbach, Darwin, Freud, Jung and William James dealt mortal blow after blow to the old transcendence model.

But there remained some voices which wouldn't be silenced or sidelined. Paul Tillich taught that God was embedded in symbols as "human creations of meaning": "God does not exist. He is being itself beyond essence and existence. Therefore to argue that God exists is to deny him". Very Denis! Dietrich Bonhoeffer envisaged a "religionless Christianity" in which, by love, we suffer for each other as Jesus suffered for others, each of us the suffering servant, "God in human form". Very Feuerbach, very Fox! In New Zealand the Presbyterian pastor Lloyd Geering was tried (and acquitted) in the 1960s for preaching Christian humanism, and in the United States Thomas Altizer reached back to Blake to proclaim an apocalyptic "gospel of Christian atheism". Here in Britain, a suffragen bishop no less, John Robinson, popularised some of these ideas in the (in)famous *Honest to God*, which celebrated the God-in rather than the God-beyond, and dared to do so in cheap paperback[6]. More recently, Anthony Freeman was sacked from his church post for a book he gave the Friendly title *God in Us*.

So we are looking not at some new postmodern fad but at a long tradition on the margins of Christianity where God and the divine have been understood as in some way intrinsic to the human condition and the human enterprise, rather than over and above it, located in some woolly-beyondness, distinct and independent of mere humankind. In its more cautious form (which would include the Quaker mainstream) the tradition has done no more than emphasise or privilege the immanence of God over his transcendence. At its most radical (Winstanley, Blake, Feuerbach, Altizer, Cupitt) it denies metaphysical transcendence altogether (which is not to say that there is no sense in which God may be understood as a symbol of "otherness" - a point to which I shall return).

For the nineteenth and most of the twentieth century the churches and religious institutions were able to hold radical immanentism at arm's length, aware of its challenge but able to muster the still substantial forces of Authority and Tradition to keep it firmly in its place on the outer margins. There were powerful vested interests at stake. From whence came the authority and power of priest and mullah, minister and elder, prophet and guru, scripture and books of discipline, if not from a transcendent objective God? What separated the religious from the secular, the spiritual from the temporal, if not a God Almighty, a God with "his" own will and purpose, a God who is himself the eternal foundation of sound values? The spectre of moral anarchy, of nihilism, was invoked as the inevitable alternative to the simplistically "real" God, and as the awful consequence of taking leave of him. And so institutional religion - not excluding the Society of Friends - pulled up its drawbridge and survived, after a fashion, the assaults and seismic upheavals of the pre-postmodern age, greatly weakened in numbers and authority, increasingly irrelevant for millions who rightly sensed that this was nonsense, but still there to fight yesterday's battles and defiantly unfurl the-day-before-yesterday's banners.

Then in the 1960s and early 70s came the cultural shift that seemed suddenly to make even the modern out-moded: the shift into what began to be called postmodernity. The quite distinct disciplines of anthropology, comparative cultural studies, comparative religion, linguistic philosophy, semiology and consciousness studies converged on a single blindingly obvious idea: there are many cultures, and no pre-given criteria for determining which is "true" and which is "false". And you didn't have to be an academic: the woman on the Selly Oak omnibus could see it with her own eyes, and so could her husband, without even lifting his eyes from the *Sun*.

In the space of a single generation, Britain became a multi-cultural, multi-faith society. We not only read about other cultures, we invaded them on package holidays, bought their food from our local take-aways, watched their conflicts on television and listened to their music on our walk-persons. And the penny dropped: our culture, our religion, our God, was one of many. How could we possibly claim that it was in any objective sense "truer" than the others? That God's truth was Christian and Quaker rather than Hindu, Buddhist or Moony? Our arts and sciences, our customs and practices, our games and rituals, our beliefs and values, the "manners of a marquis and the morals of a Methodist", all were born, bred and nourished within a particular human culture. We cannot confidently point to anything that is pre-given, foundational, known or knowable to us outside our culturally-created language - except perhaps our own humanity, whatever that might consist of.

This popular cultural revolution coincided with another seismic shift. For nearly two thousand years Western thought had been dominated by Plato's dualisms: the real and the shadow, eternal and temporal, spirit and matter, mind and body, metaphysical and physical, supernatural and natural. Classic Christian theology itself was the apotheosis of Plato's realism, which saw Truth, Beauty, Love and Justice as ultimate realities, the predicates or qualities of Almighty Ultimate Reality itself, the transcendent God. But from the seventeenth century onwards, Platonic realism had its challengers. By the mid-twentieth century it was in deep trouble. Philosophy had taken its "linguistic turn": the growing understanding that our world, our cultures, our religious beliefs and values, our experience and understanding of our experience, our consciousness and consciousness-of-our-consciousness - is all language-built, language-encoded, language-mediated. It is with language that we make sense, create meaning. And so we come to understand that all meaning, including religious meaning, is not built into some external reality but is generated from within ourselves. Our faith, our hope, our love, our values, and of course our gods - not just those odd African and Indian deities, but our very own God too - are human creations, made in human history out of human culture and language. Come to think of it, what else could they possibly be?

Famously (or infamously), the theologian who most clearly articulated "nonrealism" (though he did not coin the term) in its postmodern sense was Don Cupitt, first in *Taking Leave of God* (1979) and then in *The Sea of Faith* (1984). He took the title of this second book (which was linked to a BBC TV series) from Matthew Arnold's haunting poem *Dover Beach*, written in the mid-19th century but presciently depicting a twentieth century living out the twilight of the gods in a world which, though seemingly "a land of dreams, So various, so beautiful, so new", nevertheless "Hath really neither joy, nor love, nor light, Nor certitude, nor peace, nor help from pain": a world resembling "a darkling plain Swept with confused alarms of struggle and flight, Where ignorant armies clash by night".

Cupitt argued that we can no longer hope to banish this sense of an empty, purposeless, pitiless universe by seeking purpose, meaning and benevolence in a transcendent mastermind. It won't wash: we woke up one morning to find that we just don't believe it any more. We have to grow up, come of age, and face the awesome reality that the only purpose, meaning and benevolence in our lives is the purpose, meaning and benevolence we insist on putting there. In the evolved species we call humanity, the universe has become conscious of itself, and through human consciousness we impose such meaning as we can on the otherwise meaningless. We impose meaning by social custom, but also and crucially by our creative imagination: our arts and sciences, our relationships and our rituals, and the values which we choose to make the foundation-stones of our lives, projected as the gods of our myths and stories, scriptures and faith-practices.

The keenest criticism of postmodern theology is that once we come to see God as "nonreal" or wholly subjective, no more (but, gloriously, no less) than an objectification of human values and aspirations, we lose a God with whom we can have *relationship*: to whom we can pray, whom we can love, by whom we can be saved. This is Harvey Gillman's point: "If there is no relationship there is no Religious Society of Friends". He is surely right. But it is precisely because we need relationship that, in our stories, our art, our imagination, we project our values and aspirations on an imagined *personal* God: a God of love, a God from whom all blessings flow, a God to thank or entreat, a shelter in the time of storm, a God with a will and a purpose, a God who demands (and deserves) our love, our life, our all.

Such a God does not have to be "real like the daisies": with a shape, a colour, a scent; a thing to be defined and classified. A God who is a thing, as a daisy or a star or an antelope is a thing, is really pretty small beer. Our God can be "real like I love you" - *and there is nothing more real than "I love you"*. The child in Janet's story knew that. A child's love for her parents is the most real thing in her life - until, when she grows up, she has the even more intense experience of saying "I love you" to her lover. To love and be loved is as real as it comes. To declare love, share love, make love, is to get real. Every poet knows it, from Sappho to Shelley and Herrick to Hughes; every song-writer, from Schubert to Paul McCartney; every artist, every lover, every beloved.

Love is so real that it makes other realities seem unreal. When it happens to us, it assaults the "I" that we think we are. Listen to Jeanette Winterson: "Falling in love challenges the reality to which we lay claim; part of the pleasure of love and part of its terror is the world turned upside down. We want and we don't want, the cutting edge, the upset, the new views".

And again: "Falling in love can cause in us seismic shocks that will, if we let them, help to re-evaluate what things matter, what things we take for granted. This is frightening, and as we get older it is harder to face such risks to the deadness that we are..."

To declare love, share love, make love, is to get real.

I want to emphasise here that I am not merely labouring to restate the orthodoxy that "God is love", still less suggesting that God is reducible to child-and-parent love, or even the seismic shock of lovers' love. Too many cults have followed this seductively reductionist road and concluded that God is sex, drugs and rock-and-roll, whose sacrament is a good orgasm. I am saying that "I love you", the most awesome commitment one person can ever make to another, three words that reinvent the world, offers us a quite different kind and quality of reality from that of a flower or a mountain range, a reality that at once both transforms us and re-orders all our lesser realities. And I want to say that it is *that kind of enhanced reality* the oddly-described "nonrealist" has in mind when she reaches for what she finds she still wants to call God. The ineffable reality of "I love you", rather than the effable reality of the daisy.

What kind of theology does "real like I love you" produce? First of all, a *relationship-theology*, the relationship being an all-absorbing one which turns our world upside down: a paradoxical "want and don't want". We long to become so close to the beloved that we are part of them and they are part of us - but not identical with us, since it is clearly not ourselves we are in love with. We want to be as close as it is possible to be; to take the other into ourselves; to absorb and be absorbed - and yet remain distinct, "one" and "other". So is "real like I love you", then, a way of interpreting our God-talk as love for the only *other* who can simultaneously be *other* and the very depths of our own being? Doesn't this tell us something about immanence and transcendence, about the way we can visualise our imagined God as both in-us and beyond-us, both us and other?

Secondly, "real like I love you" suggests a *self-transforming theology*: an eager, gladsome-minded giving over of power to be affected by the beloved: a willingness to be made and remade by their needs, joys, sorrows: made and remade in relationship. This is so both when our beloved is "real like the daisies", a present, material person to be caressed with material hands, and when he/she has no present material reality: one we love who is dead or far away, or a poet's fiction, or a "virtual" lover who has seduced our imagination. Both kinds of lover, both kinds of beloved, can speak to our condition, make and remake us, reimagine us. Doesn't this tell us something about the place of imagination - the very essence of our human selves - in our quest for meaning and readiness for transformation?

Thirdly, "real like I love you" suggests a *performance theology*, a theology of the deed. "I love you" is either the profoundest statement we ever make in our lives (however many times we make it) or a cheap cheat. A real "I love you" is real by virtue of action and performance. "Love demands expression. It will not stay still, stay silent, be good, be modest, be seen and not heard, no" (Jeanette Winterson again). We have to communicate love, act upon it, and take the consequences. If we don't, it won't change us, and if it doesn't change us it isn't love. It won't change us, and won't be the love of "I love you", if we seek to keep our love, and our beloved, firmly under our own control. So, another paradox: to love is to surrender control, and that means change - and change means goodbye to the safe, the stable, the eternal. We want love to be safe, stable and eternal, but if it were, would it be love? Love is vulnerable and precarious, untamed and impassioned, and that just doesn't sit easily with safety, stability and the stasis of eternity. What that suggests to me about a relationship with a God whose reality is the impassioned reality of "I love you" is a theology of living dangerously, an *adventurous theology*, a *risk-all theology*.

Fourthly, "real like I love you" means an *aspirational theology* which calls us out of ourselves. It calls us to see better things in others and to be better ourselves. It demands that we be more than we have been, and that we enable the beloved to be more than they have been, too. This is the extravagance and generosity and beauty and awe and wonder of "real like I love you". Another Jeanette Winterson quote for the collection: "Whatever it is that pulls the pin, that hurls you past the boundaries of your own life into a brief and total beauty, even for a moment, it is enough".

So there's the beginning of a positive theology of "real like I love you". And

I hope it indicates that the nonrealist is negative only in this: she does not suppose that when she talks of God she refers to some-*thing*, an entity, an objective person or intelligence, a kind of super-daisy. She understands perfectly well that what she really experiences, really relates to, really worships, really understands to be the nature and essence of "God", is a reality comparable to that of a seismic love affair, which challenges the reality we have come to take for granted, turns our world upside down - and changes us so radically that we feel we are born again.

Matthew Arnold, even in his terrible despair at "the turbid ebb and flow Of human misery", with its "melancholy, long, withdrawing roar, Retreating to the breath Of the night-wind down the vast edges drear And naked shingles of the world", nevertheless knew the reality of "I love you": "Ah, love, let us be true To one another!" he pleads, in the one gleam of light flashing through his god-forsaken universe. (He was, I believe, on honeymoon in Dover when he wrote the poem!).

Here, then, is a God no sceptical scientist or materialist can destroy! To those who offer us the selfish gene as the meaning of life, we counter-offer a wholly human web of meaning, real like I love you. And to those who wrestle with "the problem of evil" - how can God be omnipotent and yet allow such pain and suffering and misery? - we offer not a God-thing presiding over a world which "hath really neither joy, nor love, nor light, nor certitude, nor peace, nor help from pain", but a God-experience made and continually remade by the creative imagination to lighten our darkness and ease our pain: the God who is real like I love you, and can therefore change us and change the world, as no ikon, idol, wispy spirit or daisy-daisy god can ever do.

Jeanette Winterson (a rather unQuakerly writer who has nevertheless offered some Friendly thoughts to this paper) comments: "The realist (from the Latin *res* = thing) who thinks he deals in things and not images... is not the practical man but a man caught in a fantasy of his own unmaking. The realist unmakes the coherent multiple world into a collection of random objects. He thinks of reality as that which has an objective existence, but understands no more about objective existence than that which he can touch and feel, sell and buy... The earth is not flat and neither is reality. Reality is continuous, multiple, simultaneous, complex, abundant and partly invisible. The imagination alone can fathom this" [7].

Theological realists sometimes insist that only their kind of realism is real: that those who find that an objective, transcendent God does not speak to their condition or fit their honest experience have no place in the religious community. Nonrealists take a less exclusive view. They do not for one moment seek to deny "real like the daisies" believers their place in the church or meeting, but they urge that the circle be wide enough to include those for whom God is "real like I love you". A loving, supportive meeting can welcome realist and nonrealist together, each with a different experience to offer, each willing to learn from the other. Where there is such openness it may still be possible to find an inclusive theology for the postmodern age.

And that is surely what our theology has to be about. Quaker theology should not be a poring over Quaker runes to discern a peculiarly Quaker truth. Traditional Christian theology in the academy may be closely tied to study of the Christian scriptures and the doctrines derived therefrom, but Quaker theology is a poor silly gospel if it is nothing more than a textual analysis of first and seventeenth century writings, carried out in the hope that such scrutiny will reveal a real True Quakerism or the real Quaker Truth. Contemporary theology is about contemporary *logia* of *theos*: an enquiry into what "words about God", God-language, means *today*; about how we can usefully and meaningfully continue to talk about "God" in a postmodern world where objective gods are as dead as the devil and the whole dead mythology of a separate spirit world.

Quaker theology is just theology done by Quakers (and their fellow-travellers like me), coming as they do from a distinctive tradition. This happens to be a tradition of openness, of radical questioning, of distaste for dogma, rejection of traditional authority, scepticism about creeds and formularies, spiritual bloody-mindedness and a dogged insistence on privileging personal experience over second-hand learning. Early Friends declared themselves the sons of God, no messing. The Quaker tradition emphasises the inner light of conscience rather than rules of behaviour imposed from without, a God within rather than a God-remote. I think this makes Quakers peculiarly well fitted to do contemporary theology: they arguably discovered postmodernity before the postmodernists beached their boats on Dover's "moon-blanched sand". It is not surprising that Quakers are so strongly represented in the Sea of Faith movement, which does postmodern theology by exploring what it means to understand religious faith as a human creation, or that Cupitt, though once and always an Anglican, writes in *The Future of the Church* and *The Religion of Being* that institutional Christianity needs to become more like Quakerism if it is to survive.

If God were "real like the daisies", a fixed, absolute, objective Truth, theology would have to be about discovering the truth about Truth, peeling it off layer by layer till we reach QED: an activity analogous to science. But if God is "real like I love you", God is "the human form divine", living and reigning in the human imagination. And if God and religious faith are, in the end, wholly human concepts and constructs, theology is not about discovering the truth about Truth but about *making* truth, *creating* meaning and purpose: an activity more closely analogous to the work of the imaginative creative artist than to the dogged search for the Loch Ness monster. Michael Tippett in his Third Symphony urges us: "What if the dream crack? Remake it!". If *we* made religious faith, and find it has gone sour on us, *we* can remake it - as Fox and Friends remade it in the seventeenth century - to speak to our new-millennium condition.

Isn't that what Quaker theology is *really* about? And if the remaking becomes a renewing, so that the Society and the Church, Quakerism and Christianity, change in the course of the twentyfirst century into something fresh and new, perhaps far beyond anything of which we can now conceive, we might yet find ways, looking to that of God in everyone, of transforming our world from Arnold's "darkling plain" to his "land of dreams, So various, so beautiful, so new". That remains our mobilising dream - and mobilising dreams are what theology is there to provide.

References, sources and notes:

[1] I would like to thank those who have commented on and helped me improve earlier drafts of this paper: Harvey Gillman for responding generously to the way I have taken his words out of their fuller context, thereby over-simplifying his argument; participants in the November 1998 QTS working weekend, particularly David Adshead and Rachel Muers, for their kindly but trenchant criticisms; and Alison Webster for re-introducing me to Jeanette Winterson, and working with me to develop the implications of a "real like I love you" theology.

[2] The Jeanette Winterson quotes are from her fiction *Gut Symmetries*, *Written on the Body* and *Art and Lies*, and her collection of essays *Art Objects*, all published in paperback by Vintage.

[3] *Witness to the Beast*, E.P.Thompson

[4] *The Letters of John Keats*, ed. H.C.Rollins (Cambridge, Mass), Vol 1 p184.

[5] See *A History of God*, Karen Armstrong (Heinemann) p148

[6] For Tillich see *Religion and Culture: Essays in Honor of Paul Tillich* (1959); for Bonhoeffer and Robinson *Honest to God* (Penguin, 1963); for Geering *Tomorrow's God* (Bridget Williams, Wellington NZ).

[7] Note how for Jeanette Winterson a realist must necessarily be "he", "a man". Realism is literal, logical, reasonable, common-sense: *male*. Nonrealism is imaginative, metaphorical, intuitive: *female*. So much for the common notion of nonrealism as cerebral, dispassionate, and patriarchal!

The Continuing Quest for a Reasonable Faith: Friends and the New Millennium

This paper was delivered at the 1995 Manchester Conference, organised by Hardshaw East Monthly Meeting to commemorate the 1895 Manchester Conference commonly regarded as a key event in the transition of the Society of Friends in Britain from conservatism to liberalism. About 300 Friends attended the 1995 event from all over Britain, and from Ireland, Europe and the USA.

In this paper, I invited Friends to project themselves into the future and imagine that they were meeting in the year 2095...

On this November evening in the year 2095 Common Era I propose to look back at our Society, first as it was two centuries ago and then as it was a hundred years later: at the searchings for a "reasonable faith" which came to the fore at the Manchester conference of 1895, and at the continuing quest at the time of the centenary conference in 1995.

The 1895 Manchester conference is commonly seen as something of a revolutionary moment in the history of what had become a rather un-revolutionary sect. In truth, we know that what happened then was a good deal less sudden and abrupt than some later twentieth-century Friends thought it to be. The young Turks of the Manchester conference didn't come from nowhere: they built their coup on a ground-swell of liberalism. And of course, although I have used the word "coup", there was no sudden change of leadership, nor even any immediate repudiation of evangelical dogmas and pieties. It took the Society at large some years to catch up with what John Wilhelm Rowntree, William Charles Braithwaite, Rendel Harris and their comrades had done here in Manchester in November 1895.

What exactly had they done? It is generally accepted that they cemented the foundations of the liberal, undogmatic, doctrinally easygoing Society of the succeeding century. They came to be seen as the founding fathers (founding mothers were not quite so much to the fore then) of a new radical Quakerism, a Quakerism which broke with evangelical orthodoxies and substituted for them a more open-minded, more rational, more modern, approach to religious and moral issues.

I have laid some emphasis on the words "radical" and "modern". But I want to ask: *how* radical, *how* modern, were the ideas of 1895? First, what were these ideas?

Twenty-seven-year-old John Wilhelm Rowntree, in a conference session titled "Has Quakerism a message to the world today?", argued that Friends should "study the dark problems of poverty... and give our teaching the force of applied Christianity". This was widely understood as the advocacy of socialism. He also put forward a concept of progressive development in social ideas and in religious thought: "The Church exists to create for each succeeding generation the ideal of the Christ in the thought-form of the age." This was widely understood as the acceptance of progressive revelation, or religious evolution: a concept clearly allied to the biological evolutionism of Charles Darwin. Where orthodoxy had posited a fixed religious Truth, beginning with an historical act of Creation, the radicals argued that Truth evolved, just as Darwin had shown that life itself was an evolutionary process.

In another conference session titled "The attitude to modern thought", Rowntree's allies developed these ideas. As Roger Wilson commented nearly a century later, "modern thought" was itself "a code-word used to link Darwinian Evolution, Scientific Research and Higher Biblical Criticism". So Rendel Harris openly embraced "the doctrine of evolution", which, he insisted, "[is] not going to be restricted to protoplasm and zoology; it is just as applicable to Scriptures, to Churches, and to Sacraments, and will tell us just as romantic tales in interpreting the growth of these as... in the study of the lowest forms of animal life."

Socialism, Darwinism and Biblical criticism: an unholy trinity to conservative believers. But how new, how radical, how modern was this assault on traditional religion? It seems clear enough that the young men who launched the assault in fervour, and the old who listened in horror, both believed that something very new, very radical and very modern was unleashed that day in Manchester. With the benefit of hindsight, we can have no such illusion.

John Wilhelm Rowntree's social gospel can now be recognised as a fairly innocuous reiteration of traditional Quaker social concern. Indeed, compared with George Fox's calls for the abolition of the aristocracy and his demand that all great estates, church properties and Whitehall itself be confiscated and redistributed to the poor, Rowntree's call for the problems of poverty to be merely "studied" seems cautious to the point of Blairism. But what alarmed conservative Friends was that Rowntree's rhetoric seemed to carry echoes of socialism. Well of course it did: the Independent Labour Party had been formed only two years earlier under Keir Hardie, and socialism was part of the intellectual and cultural ethos of the age. But it was nothing new. Socialism in Britain had a 70-year history by 1895, from Robert Owen, through Chartism, Marxism, Labour representation in Parliament from the 1870s and the new trades unionism of the 1880s. Even within the churches its pedigree was as long, if not longer, from the Christian communism of Bishop Claude Fauchet during the French revolution to the Christian Socialist movement founded by Kingsley and Maurice in the 1840s. Peterloo, which could be said to have given birth to British socialism, happened literally just across the road from where we are meeting today (Mount Street meetinghouse), and the wounded were tended in the previous meetinghouse on this site. That was 76 years before Rowntree discovered socialism.

Then there was the evolutionism espoused by Rendel Harris. This too was hardly new. Organic evolution as a theory of species origination had begun with George Fox's Quaker contemporary John Ray and had been well elaborated by Erasmus Darwin and J. B. Lamarck by the early nineteenth century, attracting no great concern among traditional creationists, who had little trouble in conceding that God's creative process could conceivably have been a little slower than Genesis 1 seemed to suggest. Charles Darwin had certainly upset the apple-cart by marshalling evidence, in *Origin of Species*, that the mechanism of evolution was impersonal natural selection rather than conscious divine will; but that was way back in 1859. The great debate between Thomas Huxley and Bishop Samuel Wilberforce, seen in its time to epitomise the struggle between old religion and new science, was 35 years in the past at the time of the Manchester conference. Darwinism was old hat to the rising generation of the 1880s and 1890s.

If neither a touch of socialist rhetoric nor a sliver of Darwinian science were exactly at the cutting edge of modern thought by 1895, no more was Biblical criticism. After all, had not Quakers virtually invented it, and a long time ago, too? Since the revolutionary 1640s, Quakers and their immediate predecessors on the Reformation Left had challenged the superstition that the Jewish and Christian scriptures were the infallible, incorruptible Word of God, the ultimate authority on doctrine and behaviour. Samuel Fisher in the 1650s subjected the Biblical text to critical analysis, treating it as a book like any other. He thought it was read too much and heard too often. Nor was this an oddity from Quakerism's ranting tendency: Fisher was a close friend of Fox, and William Penn endorsed "the truth and reasonableness of those principles he defended". Fisher's complete *Works* remained a Quaker textbook well into the eighteenth century - and would repay study today, if you can take his language, which was tortuous even by the standards of his day.

But even if the early radical Quaker tradition had faded by the 1890s (weighty evangelical Friends had probably never heard of Fisher), the so-called modern "higher criticism" of nineteenth-century scholarship had reached its own zenith long before Manchester. English translations of the Koran as early as the 1640s and the Bhagavad Gita in 1785 had long made the reading public aware that there were other scriptures beside the Christian canon. By the mid-eighteenth century the Hebrew scholar Bishop Robert Lowth was explaining the nature of Old Testament poetry, recognising it as the composition of bardic story-tellers, compiled layer upon layer over several generations. By the 1790s, let alone the 1890s, it was widely accepted among scholars that Genesis, for instance, was not written by a single divinely-inspired historical Moses, but was the work of several hands and the collation of several myths. By this time, Joseph Johnson's periodical, the *Analytical Review*, was carrying regular commentaries on the latest Biblical research, and a visionary like William Blake felt free to read the Bible as literature and pillage it for his own divinely inspired poetry, conferring his own meaning on it rather than searching its texts for hidden messages dictated by God in the remote past.

German Lutherans were soon travelling the same road. D. F. Strauss published his two-volume *The Life of Jesus Critically Examined* in 1835. The English translation followed in 1846. (The translator, incidentally, was George Eliot, who thus had the double distinction of writing a fictional masterpiece in *Middlemarch* and bringing to an English-speaking audience the century's most important theological book.) In the 1840s Ludwig Feuerbach published his first work offering a humanist interpretation of the Christian texts. In 1859 the *Codex Sinaiticus* was discovered, revolutionising Biblical textual studies. In the same year (which also saw publication of *Origin of Species*) young Quakers began meeting in the new Manchester Institute to discuss these matters (much against the wishes of their elders and Elders), and 24-year-old John Stephenson Rowntree published a prize essay attributing the decline of Quakerism to its hostility to thinking and its disparagement of the lively mind. In 1860 an Anglican volume with the

innocuous and unrevealing title *Essays and Reviews* upset those who read little
and thought less by suggesting that Biblical stories such as the one about
Balaam's talking ass could be understood as legends. By the year of the
Manchester conference the heresies of *Essays and Reviews* were well on the
way to becoming Anglican orthodoxies, and one of the book's authors,
Frederick Temple, was Bishop of London, and a year later Archbishop of
Canterbury. What had happened was that liberalism, including free Biblical
criticism, had taken its place as an accepted wing of the churches. (I might
add that this process of abandonment of the old verities by the educated
classes had been anticipated by the working class, which lost faith in old-style
religion long before the intellectuals cottoned on.)

So you get my drift: by invoking the language of socialism, Darwinism and
Biblical criticism Rowntree, Harris and company may have seemed
outrageous radicals to Quaker evangelicals, but in the wider world of
thinking, reading, cultured men and women they were not at the cutting
edge of modern thought. A little late in the day, they had caught up with the
new ideas which had shaken mainstream social and religious institutions
more than half a century earlier. Now they were invoking yesterday's buzz
words to shake up the Society of Friends. In 1895, with only five years of the
nineteenth century to go, they sought to drag their beloved Society into it.

You will perhaps think I am being a little unfair. Were even the most
advanced thinkers at the 1895 Manchester conference really behind rather
than ahead of their times? I think they were, for the reasons I have given, but
I have no wish to challenge the common perception that the Society did have
its own distinctive light to shine on the darkness. Quakers generally were
ahead of their times in their opposition to slavery, their hostility to violence
and coercion, in their attitude to penal reform, and in their compassionate
approach to mental illness. Earlier generations of Friends had pioneered
radical opposition to clerical authority and Biblical tyranny, even if much of
their pioneering spirit was dormant by the nineteenth century. Most
important of all, the steadfastness of seventeenth-century Friends "for
conscience' sake" had opened the way to toleration of dissent, and thus to
religious and political pluralism: the single biggest contribution Quakers
ever made to human progress. I don't under-value any of this. But I do say
that we can over-blow our own trumpets. And if we suppose that the
Manchester liberals were at the cutting edge of "modern thought" we kid
ourselves. Enlightened and progressive in comparison with their
obscurantist evangelical Friends, of course: but ever so moderate, if not just

a bit old-fashioned, compared with their radical contemporaries.

The scene doesn't look so very different to me when I leap a hundred years to 1995! The twentieth century saw change on a scale even the most visionary minds of the Victorian age could never have dreamt of. The revolutions in transport and communications, electronics and technology, which literally changed the face of the earth, were matched by revolutions in the understanding of human psychology and consciousness, in politics, philosophy and theology. Friends led in none of these fields; in fact, they were often slow to catch up. They remained prominent in some forms of social action: the struggle for recognition of conscientious objection to military service, the long campaign against weapons of mass destruction, the organisation of famine relief, campaigns to free prisoners of conscience and to stop torture. But in the hard task of developing a theology to match the age, Friends, despite their often complacent view of themselves as "progressive" (in moderation), often seemed to lag some way behind thinkers from the supposedly more conservative mainstream traditions.

In the 1860s the poet Matthew Arnold had stood on Dover beach listening to the "melancholy, long, withdrawing roar" of the receding Sea of Faith, "retreating, to the breath of the night-wind, down the vast edges drear and naked shingles of the world". If the tide of organised faith had begun to go out in the nineteenth century, it continued to ebb away throughout the twentieth. "Modern thought" demoted God, but postmodern thought seemed to depose him altogether. After the revolutions in science, psychology and, most important of all, the understanding of language, humankind came to know that "no saviour from on high delivers". What we had thought was eternal could only be provisional, what seemed absolute had to be relative. Where did that leave the Truth published by Fox and his "Valiant Sixty", and presented in fresh clothes by the Manchester reformers? Where did it leave the "universal truth" supposed to be at the core of all religions and faith traditions?

Well into the twenty-first century, millions refused to be parted from the comforting certainties, their ancient authorities. They found in traditional fundamentalisms - Christian, Muslim, Jewish - a refuge from the terrifying burden of liberty with which postmodernism seemed to threaten them. Millions more abandoned dead fundamentalisms without ever finding anything to replace them. But there were some who sought to refashion faith in the age of relativity and subjectivity. Few, to begin with, were Quakers -

despite the fact that Quakerism was founded on the authority of experience, and experience has to be relative and subjective. The Religious Society of Friends as a whole was as reluctant as most institutions to expose its most cherished formulations to the light of the twentieth century's laser beams, and to subject its own acquired language to the radical deconstruction (which does not mean destruction or denigration) demanded by a new understanding of how language works.

So the earliest moves towards an expressionist, humanist or non-realist religious faith were made not by Friends, but by detached thinkers like Ludwig Wittgenstein, and developed by Anglican theologians like John Robinson and, more radically, Don Cupitt. They grasped that all religious faith - Catholic and Moony, Hindu and Native American, Rastafarian and Quaker, conservative and liberal - is created in human culture and by human imagination, matured in human history and celebrated in human language and human community.

Community. And here I want to emphasise that my confessed readiness to accept the twentieth- and twenty-first-century view that religious values are wholly human, that we must learn to get along without an absolute referent, since even our supposed absolutes need human interpretation, and interpretation is inevitably conditioned by human culture and history, must not be confused with privatised religion, or misunderstood as a surrender to the spirit of the age as expressed in the worship of its almighty god Free Market Forces. Values generated in human community are the exact opposite of all that. They are its deadliest enemy.

Because faith without works is dead, Quakerism without a living social testimony - a testimony which was at the core of levelling, republican Quakerism in 1652 - doesn't deserve to live. What shall it profit a man to save his own precious soul - the ultimate privatisation - and do nothing to mend the world?

But... I don't believe we'll advance towards the Kingdom (I'd rather say Commonwealth) of Heaven by retreating to a nineteenth-century, or seventeenth-century or first-century theology, by settling for yesterday's models of God and Truth if we can no longer hold them with integrity. The Commonwealth of Heaven will be built brick by brick in this profoundly complicated world as we absorb the lesson that truth is diverse, truth is plural - and that is the truth that makes us free.

We know what we have to confront: the religion of "There is no such thing as society". But in rejecting that as the spirit of the age, we must not make the mistake of rejecting the age itself. We have learnt so much, and have so much to learn. We cannot put the clock back.

The new understanding of religion, of which I have been speaking, the understanding of religion as wholly human, seems blindingly obvious from our late twenty-first-century vantage point. But, like the Quakerism of the 1650s, it was denounced in the 1990s as "atheism" and "blasphemy", or put down as sceptical reductionism or mere intellectual "notions". Nevertheless, there were Friends who were joyfully relating their wholly subjective and metaphorical understanding of God not only to the exclusively experiential nature of the faith of George Fox, James Nayler and Isaac Penington, but to William Blake: "Mercy, Pity, Peace and Love is God" - and is human too, "For Mercy has a human heart, Pity a human face, and Love the human form divine, and Peace a human dress". That is "the human form divine". "All deities", Blake added, "reside in the human breast".

Our own twenty-first century saw the deepening divide between premodern objective religion, where the natural and the supernatural diced with each other, and a postmodern subjective faith which carried forward the seventeenth-century Quaker project of wholly and radically incarnating God in the human spirit, dispersing the divine into humanity, extinguishing the old natural/supernatural dualism, and centring spirituality on human experience. From the 1990s, and on into the twenty-first century, Friends, along with the rest of the Christian tradition, and other faith traditions too, had to wrestle with this new light, which turned out to be only a fresh beam from the old Light of the World, powered by recharged batteries.

Just as Manchester 1895 belatedly caught the liberal spirit of the age and saved the Society of Friends from a slow dying of the light, so the Friends who gathered together in the same city and same meeting-house in 1995 found themselves facing the same task: to fashion a reasonable faith for a new century and a new millennium. They couldn't foresee the result. If only we could step back a hundred years, and tell them!

The Diversity of Truth

This paper was delivered to the 1995 Quaker Theology Seminar on "Truth and Diversity" and was reprinted in "Searching the Depths", edited by Harvey Gillman and Alastair Heron (Quaker Home Service, 1996). I have made a few corrections to the QHS version.

Given the diversity of opinions among Quakers, is it still possible to talk of "the one Truth we witness to"? This question was posed recently by the Quaker Theology Seminar and inevitably several responses were on offer.

A good starting point is that word "still". It implies that there really was a time when Quakers could talk meaningfully of "the one Truth" to which they bore common witness: a golden age of unity when the Society spoke with one voice, with each member led in the same direction to the same conclusion, the same theology, the same witness. But was there ever such a heavenly harmony? If there was, Quaker historians have yet to locate it.

A hundred years ago, perhaps in our fathers' and grandfathers' day? Read the letters columns in *The Friend* of the 1920s and 30s to find that controversy and genteel Quakerly bickering is no new postmodern phenomenon. The nineteenth century? Re-read Roger Wilson's *Manchester, Manchester and Manchester Again* for a chilling reminder of the passionate divisions between "sound doctrine" Quakers and liberals in England. When David Duncan, a leading spokesman for the liberals, died suddenly of smallpox just as the controversy threatened to split the Society, John Bevan Braithwaite, weightiest of the weighty evangelicals, wrote in his diary, "How wonderful are the ways of providence!".

The eighteenth century, then? When it comes to controversy, the age of cocoa Quakerism turns out to have been rather less soporific than the much misused term "quietism" suggests. Tucked away in their own little world of drab dress and archaic language, the advocates of silent worship battled against preaching Friends, with much party squabbling on the true meaning of Truth. In North America, these practical and theological divisions split the Society into competing sects. In Britain they simmered in the same pot, but gave off no less steam.

The pioneers, then: surely *they* had a grasp of one Truth, one common witness? Alas for golden age dreamers, they did not. Gerrard Winstanley, thought by some to be "leader of the Quakers" before Fox's ascendancy, taught that God was Reason and the Bible wholly mythological. As early as 1651 Fox encountered Quakers who followed Rhys Jones in arguing that it was not necessary to believe in an historical Jesus, and Fox remained troubled by the Rhys Jones tendency for the rest of his life. John Perrot and his supporters thought Fox did not go far enough in breaking with established religious and social tradition, and took a more radical view of the equality of women. Others, of course, thought the Fox-Fell axis gave women too much scope. Samuel Fisher's sweeping biblical criticism - two hundred years ahead of the German scholars who are supposed to have invented it - horrified some within the fold, as did William Penn's politicking with the Catholic James II. There were those who thought slave-trading and slave-holding inconsistent with Truth, and those who thought God required only that slaves be properly treated (provided they knew their place, behaved themselves and, as Fox exhorted them, loved their masters). Some held Fox to be uniquely inspired, others (Quakers, not outsiders) reviled him as the "Quaker Pope".

There are latter-day Friends (such is our diversity even in the matter of Quaker history) who question whether some of those I have called to the witness box may properly be described as Quakers. The point is an important one. If we do acknowledge them as part of the early Quaker family, early diversity is abundantly demonstrated. If we don't, I am writing bad history and advancing a poor argument. So let us investigate.

We first encounter a problem. Although some meetings began compiling lists of names in the early 1650s, there was not for many years any official membership, nor even any formal Society to belong to. "Quaker" was thus an imprecise term. We can choose, if we wish, to regard as Quakers only those who accepted Fox's ascendancy; or, less prejudicially, we can simply say that before there was any Quaker organisation the term Quakers can be applied to those antinomian and anti-clerical separatists who were "called in scorn Quakers" by their opponents, or who called themselves Quakers, or whose writings plainly reflect contemporary Quaker apologetics. Some of those I cite were Quakers in Fox's terms, and belonged to the inner circle as it became a formal Society (for example, Samuel Fisher and William Penn). Others belonged to tendencies which, though they lost out in the ideological and personal battles which were eventually won by Fox and his followers, were "Quaker" nonetheless.

Rhys Jones was a former Baptist dramatically convinced by Fox in 1651. According to an undated memorandum by Oliver Hooton (cited by Larry Ingles in *First Among Equals*) he embraced Fox and told him that "the Lord had a mighty work through and by him". Jones led a Nottingham group of "Children of Light", as early Quakers called themselves, and in correspondence between Fox and others in 1654 is clearly regarded as a member of the flock, albeit a troublesome one. Jones and his followers subsequently formed the nucleus of the "Proud Quaker" tendency, but Quakers still, by any definition except the narrowest which reserves the term exclusively for Fox's following.

John Perrot was acknowledged as a gifted member of the early Quaker leadership. Edward Burrough called him "eminent in the nation". Fox himself praised Perrot's Quaker missionary work in Rome in his 1658 pamphlet *An Answer to a Paper which came from the Papists*, as well he may have done, since Perrot was captured and tortured by the Inquisition, shackled by the neck and regularly flogged with a dried bull's penis, which treatment seems to have driven him half-mad. But Perrot, like Jones and James Nayler before him, was perceived as an alternative leader, particularly when Quaker women rallied behind his more thorough-going defence of women's equality in the movement. Fox set out to destroy his authority, and did so.

Samuel Fisher's credentials as a true Quaker have never been questioned. Another former Baptist and one of the few university-educated Quakers, he remained a friend and associate of Fox from his convincement in 1654. What I have called his "sweeping biblical criticism" is demonstrated in his brilliant *A Rustics Alarm to the Rabbies* of 1660, in which he mocks the idea that the Bible is the Word of God or uniquely inspired. The Apocrypha and various lost Gospels (some to be rediscovered in our own time), even the Koran, he says, could make an equally plausible claim to divine inspiration. This goes somewhat beyond Fox's own doctrine that the biblical canon witnessed to the Word though it was not the Word itself, but Fisher was never publicly challenged or repudiated by Fox, though his radicalism clearly embarrassed some Quakers, who gave more prominence to his less provocative works than to the *Rustics Alarm*. Christopher Hill writes in *The World Turned Upside Down* that "Fisher virtually abandoned hope of unity of interpretation, and so of any external unity. It is the end of the authority of the Book; but by no means a return to the authority of tradition. It is simply the end of authority... Fisher deserves greater recognition as a precursor of the English enlightenment than he has yet received"

Gerrard Winstanley is a more difficult case. Edward Burrough met the "True Leveller" leader in 1654, and reported to Swarthmoor Hall (Margaret Fell's home near Ulverston, already the working base for Fox's "Valiant Sixty"): 'Winstanley says he believes we are sent to perfect that work which fell into their hands - he hath been with us'. Winstanley's 1640s writings prefigured 1650s Quaker writings in so many ways (though they were far more radical) that only those who cannot stomach his communism and rationalism would wish to disown him (much as post-Restoration Quakers took every opportunity to distance themselves from any hint of "levelling"). The Leveller leader John Lilburne became a Quaker, but promptly died before his political past became an issue. Available evidence suggests that Winstanley (whose non-violent occupation of common land at St. George's Hill, Surrey, is being commemorated and repeated by latter-day True Levellers even as I write) did the same for a while, perhaps till he found Quakers too conservative for him, at which point he seems to have abandoned controversy and taken up gardening. One knows the feeling!

By the 1660s and 1670s, not only were there the fringe Quaker groups such as "Proud Quakers" and the "refined Quakers" in the last remnants of the Family of Love, but Friends within mainstream Quakerism were defining parties among themselves, as "Foxonian", "King George Fox'", "G. Fox and his Party", "our Quaker Pope". If there was "one truth they witnessed to", it was a diverse truth indeed. In these momentous upheavals, the movement (or church, or sect) struggled to reconcile its founding faith in individual experience and conscience with a perceived need to "witness to one Truth". Fox had asked "What canst thou say?'" in the full expectation that the thou he was addressing would be led by the spirit to say much the same as he, Fox, was saying. To his bewilderment and frustration, the thou sometimes said something different. Who was to decide which was Truth? Was Fox's truth Truth, or Nayler's, or Perrot's or Rhys Jones's? Fox's answer was to fall back on the very tradition he had broken with: the church must decide. What the spirit appeared to say through individuals was unreliable, but it would speak infallibly through the gathered meeting (which all too often meant in practice that it would voice Truth as understood by the meeting's dominant personalities, of whom none was more dominant than Fox).

Later, attempts would be made to enforce the meeting's orthodoxies through what amounted to a Quaker equivalent of the old church courts. Quaker liberty became Quaker discipline, Quaker diversity Quaker orthodoxy. I am not concerned here with the argument - a powerful one - that Fox's strategy was necessary to the Society's survival. I merely record that there never was a time, not even in the Society's glory days, when there really was "the one Truth" witnessed to by all. Indeed, a modern scholarly biography of Fox, such as H. Larry Ingle's *First among Friends*, makes it clear that the charismatic personality still sometimes inaccurately described as the "founder" of the Quaker movement spent the greater part of his life not preaching to the unconverted, but persuading, cajoling and bullying his fellow-Quakers into the orthodoxies that he called Truth. In this he resembled the apostle Paul, whose surviving writings all take the form of letters to new churches, settling arguments, averting schisms, scolding those which step out of line, and laying down a one Truth to be witnessed to. Paul and Fox: valiant for their own orthodoxy! And just as Paul's letters, in the act of condemning it, reveal the huge diversity of opinion in the early church, so Fox's letters, pamphlets and Journal reveal the extent to which early Quakers begged to differ from one another.

So the past is similar to the present. There always were wide differences of opinion among Quakers, a diversity of approaches to Truth or truths. To yearn nostalgically for a simpler, purer age of doctrinal unity is to yearn for an age that never was. Past and present do differ in that we no longer denounce and anathematise each other in the sometimes astonishingly virulent language our forebears used. Nor is it likely that, say, a latter-day Quaker evangelical would thank God for his providence in killing off a troublesome Quaker universalist opponent.   We have largely lost the overwhelming and overweening sense of certainty that sustained the pioneers - and we are surely all the better for it. For slowly and agonisingly, over the past three hundred years we have had to learn how to live with uncertainty: with the realisation that we may be mistaken and that, though there may be contingent truths and untruths, there is no absolute, unchanging religious truth, no Truth with a capital T. Truth, we have learnt, is itself diverse, and is to be made rather than found. Whatever seems to speak to our condition, to ring true, that is our truth for the time being, and will remain so until our condition changes, until new bells ring out new truths. We have a theology that no one view is absolutely "right", even the view we most cherish. Truth is relative and cultural. Of course it is. We now wonder how it could ever have been thought to be anything else.

Don Cupitt - an Anglican theologian who acknowledges the achievement of seventeenth-century Quakerism in "bringing Power down from Heaven and dispersing it into human hearts" - has charted in *The Sea of Faith* the historical breakdown of certainty, of Platonic or Aristotelian "truth", among philosophers, theologians and creative writers and thinkers from the

Enlightenment to the postmodern age. But what makes this and Cupitt's subsequent writings inspirational is the exuberant joy and delight with which he sees off the tyranny of "one Truth" and embraces the provisional. A markedly similar exuberance is also to be found in the very first Quaker writings, and that is no accident. Of course Winstanley, Rhys Jones, Perrot, Nayler, Fisher and Fox saw things very differently from the way Cupitt sees things three centuries and several philosophical and theological revolutions later. But (at least to begin with) they, like Cupitt, located ultimate authority within rather than without: the first step on the long road to relativism, which is the truth that makes us free.

What I am saying is this: The search for doctrinal unity, for truth with a capital T, is pointless because it will be fruitless. If earlier Quaker generations cobbled together a one Truth they could witness to, it was a Truth which could be maintained only by discipline, and which changed subtly from generation to generation. Quakers today are, or should be, free from tyranny of that kind of Truth: true doctrine. The spirit leads us in different directions, because our faith is experiential, and our experiences, backgrounds, temperaments, capacities differ widely. The spirit which leads us into all truths - there are a lot of them, and they never stay the same - has itself become diverse, experimental, exploratory, for we have begun to understand that this spirit is not some independent entity, external to ourselves, but one that lives and moves and has its being in the infinite diversity of our human consciousness.

Does this mean, then, that there can never be any basis whatever for any kind of Quaker unity? Surely not. It simply means that we do not need doctrinal unity or faith in a doctrinal Truth. Our unity, our group or subculture identity, depends on something different. I believe that the "something different" is the shared sense of belonging to a particular tradition, focused on the manner in which Quakers choose to meet for worship, meditation or contemplation - call it what we will. Quakers in Britain are people who choose to meet in this particular unprogrammed way, people whose current needs, preferences, temperaments, lead them to get something out of, and hopefully put something into, this particular (and rather arcane) ritual. That, and nothing more (but nothing less), is a basis of our unity. That is our bottom line.

Experience, Religious Experience and Language

This paper was written for the 1998 Quaker Theology Seminar on "Experience and Language in Quaker Theology"

We often lose sight of the fact that every verbal term or phrase we use has a history, arising and developing in a particular cultural and temporal framework. Even the words we use to describe or express or point to "things eternal" are culture-specific. (And, of course, what we think of as "things eternal" change too).

This is as true of the word/concept/idea "experience" and its qualified term "religious experience" as of anything else.

"Experience" as we have come to understand it is a relatively modern invention. Before the seventeenth century, the verb "to experience" most commonly meant "to try out, to put to the test, to experiment". The noun "experience" most commonly meant "a trial, an experiment". So an experience wasn't usually something which happened to you, something passive, but something you did, something active. This active sense of "experience" almost totally displaced the passive meaning in the late seventeenth and eighteenth centuries, when, of course, it was much reinforced by its association with the new experimental sciences. Thus "experience" (according to *The Shorter Oxford English Dictionary on Historical Principles*) is used in 1668 to mean "trial", in 1698 "an experimental fact, maxim, rule or device", in 1715 "proof by trial, demonstration", and in 1763 simply "experiment". (*Cf* G. Fox: "This I knew experimentally").

Not till the nineteenth century did "experience" fully recover its almost wholly passive sense of something which happens to us rather than something we make happen. A similar shift is detectable in the phrase "religious experience". It appears to have been born in America during the first evangelical awakenings at the end of the eighteenth century, when "to experience religion" was taken to mean experiencing "born-again" conversion. As a newly-minted phrase, "religious experience" first appears in print (according to Don Cupitt in *Mysticism after Modernity*) in 1809 in the title of a tract by an evangelical preacher, *A Diary of the Religious Experience of Mary Waring*. Half a century later, in her early novel *Scenes from Clerical*

Experience (1858), the once-evangelical author who would later write under the pseudonym George Eliot describes church-goers who "had gained a religious vocabulary rather than religious experience". "Religious experience" is clearly used in both instances to indicate an inner feeling, a state of consciousness, which meaning is familiar to us today, but was more novel then.

Cupitt suggests that the more passive sense of "experience", and particularly "religious experience", derives from the accelerating drive towards individualism and the habit of looking inwards. The early-modern period saw the collapse of church authority and the rise, first of fissile Protestantism with its competing claims to Biblical interpretation and the possession of Truth, and then of secularism and its denial of supernatural authority. If it was no longer possible to assert, let alone prove, the existence of God and a metaphysical foundation by resort to the authority of the church and holy scriptures, all that was left was an inner certainty, an intuition. Thus "religious experience" was something which you *had*, which you *received*, when the hidden God made Himself known to you by making something happen to you. "Religious experience" was internal, not something you did but something which came to you.

William James gave "religious experience" a new twist in 1902 with *The Varieties of Religious Experience*. Most of us have forgotten its sub-title: *A Study in Human Nature*. A Darwinian and pioneer of scientific psychology, James does not understand "religious experience" in the old way as something which is given to the soul from "Above" or "Beyond". For him "religious experience" is indeed internal, but generated from within, not imported from without: it is a function or capacity of human nature, just one kind of "experience" alongside "aesthetic experience" or "moral experience". The result is that "religious experience" has meant two different things through much of the twentieth century. To those who ignore James and consciously choose to retain a supernatural frame of reference, it still refers to some kind of power or knowledge or enlightenment flowing in from a divine, transcendent realm. To those for whom, after Darwin and James, a supernatural frame of reference no longer makes any sense, "religious experience" is immanent, generated from "within". James thought the varieties of psychological "religious experience" could be studied with the aim of producing a new science of religion which would strip it of supernaturalism and naturalise it.

That liberal-modern view of "religious experience" has in turn come to look dated since the 1970s, first with the publication of Stephen Katz's enormously influential studies *Mystical and Philosophical Analysis* and *Mysticism and Religious Traditions* (OUP, both 1978) and subsequently with the revolution in literary theory and linguistic philosophy generally lumped together in the inadequate term "deconstruction". Whether or not we are prepared to go all the way with Derrida and the deconstructionists, we have come to understand in the last three decades that "religious experience" is always and everywhere couched in the locally available symbolic vocabulary. Every religious experience is a datable human cultural expression. The convinced Christian will see and experience Jesus, the Hindu one of the many faces of Hindu divinity, the panentheist a "spirit that rolls through all things", the non-realist or religious humanist the wholly human values of mercy, pity, peace and love projected on to a God imagined, and fully understood to be imagined, in our own specific cultural and linguistic terms.

I would suggest that the most important insight to be had from these postmodern developments (which we cannot ignore, however unpalatable they might be to some, and however threatening to our traditional way of looking at things) is that our "experience", our "religious experience", is always encoded in words, in language. In the beginning was the word, not some wordless "experience". Of course it is possible for a language-less baby or our pet cat to "experience" pain or hunger, but to know what one is experiencing, to understand it, categorise it, find meaning in it or make meaning out of it, to analyse it, reflect on it, evaluate it, we need words. There is no such thing as wholly extra-linguistic experience, knowledge or truth. The very act of experiencing is language-built. Language goes all the way down. It's there in the great stick of rock of life wherever you cut it. There is no meaningfulness and no cognition without language. It is not just that we can't communicate properly with other human beings without language: we cannot even comprehend or communicate with ourselves without it. We cannot think at anything other than the crudest animal or baby level without words. So our "religious experience", postmodern theology and philosophy is suggesting, cannot be meaningfully separated from the words which give it a structure of meaning. (When Wordsworth said that words are the *clothing* of thoughts, Coleridge replied: "No! words are the *incarnation* of thoughts!" Coleridge was a postmodernist non-realist a century and a half ahead of his time!).

True, Paul in II Corinthians 12.4 writes (words!) about visions and revelations expressed in "unspeakable words": perhaps the origin of the paradoxical idea of unspeakable speech, "experience" beyond words. A few centuries later, in one of the most celebrated passages in his *Confessions*, Augustine writes (more words!) about a conversation (yet more words!) with his mother in which together they soar above the world and the heavens, above their own minds, above words, until, "with a sigh, we returned to the sounds of our own tongue, where the spoken word had both beginning and end". But both Paul and Augustine fail to notice that in describing the indescribable as indescribable they are describing it (describe: to deduce by words), just as when we describe a good meal as "beyond words" or a sunset as ineffable we are using the language of paradox to heighten our expression. Both Paul and Augustine are writers - wordsmiths, poets - as are all mystics. How else can you mysticise without bending, carressing, coining, expanding, subverting and overturning words, and arranging them in the sequences, patterns and rhythms which make them come alive with meaning? What is poetry but the right words in the right order? And what is mysticism, if not the same?

I have been reading a book of essays by Anglican writers called *No Discouragement*. The editor tells us that what the contributors have in common is "the recognition that language has, in the religious context, become largely useless". But it has taken them 296 pages of close-packed language to express the conviction that language is useless, and the reader is asked to pay £8.95 plus £1 p&p for a discourse expressed in this apparently useless medium!

I recognise that the post-1960s view that language and culture permeate all, that there is no pre-verbal or supra-verbal cognition of "religious experience" (a view, incidentally, which some forms of Buddhism have been comfortable with for centuries), is a challenge to a tradition like Quakerism which has come to see silence as something "beyond words", and words themselves as suspect, the product of fallible heads rather than more trustworthy hearts. It's a challenge which has to be faced squarely. The view I have described has come to hold sway in much of our postmodern culture. That doesn't mean it has to be "right", but it does mean that Quakers who reject it have to be clear on what rational and logical basis they do so. It isn't enough to say "But this isn't Quakerism" or "This isn't how I feel'.

I have quoted Don Cupitt, to whom I am indebted for helping me articulate these thoughts. (Yes, yes, I know, the thinking of the thoughts and the articulation of them *are* one process!). I would recommend his book *Mysticism after Modernity*, which discusses "experience", "religious experience" and mysticism from a postmodern perspective, where they are embraced with joy in the following terms:

"Now, with the end of metaphysics and two-worlds dualism, we should give up... the idea that mysticism is a special wordless way of intuitively knowing the things of another and higher world. We may discover that we no longer wish to go beyond. We do not hunger for "absolutes", and we are happy to give up the whole idea of equating blessedness with the gaining of a higher kind of knowledge. It is possible to be completely happy without either absolute knowledge or absolute Reality". What Cupitt calls "a mysticism of secondariness" (because we now understand that there is no primary first principle or absolute foundation from which to start) is "mysticism minus metaphysics, mysticism minus any claim to special or privileged knowledge, and mysticism without any other world than this one". This is a mysticism, a "religious experience", for the secular world which we now inhabit. And for Quakers, who have for three and a half centuries preached that the secular and the sacred are one, this is perhaps nothing new, even if the terms in which it is formulated are new to Quaker theology.

Jesus: History, Mystery or Story?

This is the revised version of a draft paper submitted to the Quaker Theology Seminar meeting in November 1995 on "The Presence in the Midst". The paper presents the argument that the historical Jesus and the mystical Jesus or Christ by themselves no longer provide us with an adequate foundation for our faith. All we can be sure of is the Jesus **story***. The paper explores what this might mean for meeting for worship and for the concept of a "presence in the midst"*

L et me start with a text: *"(Jesus) saith unto them, But whom say ye that I am? And Simon Peter answered and said, Thou art the Christ, the Son of the living God."* Matthew XVI 15-16.

According to the traditional story, Peter's reward for giving the "right" answer was the first papacy. He was to be the rock on which the church would be built, and to him was given the power to bind men's souls. So Peter's answer has echoed down twenty centuries as the definitive summation for most Christians of what Jesus means.

But even definitive summations need the occasional dusting over. The word "Jesus" is defined by other words, which tell us what "Jesus" means, but what do *they* mean? So for the same twenty centuries Christians have said "Yes, but what does 'the Christ' mean? What does 'the Son' mean? And what do we mean by 'the living God'?"

The Reformation Left of the mid-seventeenth century thought no religious question so sacrosanct that it could not be re-examined, challenged and tested anew. So it is not surprising to find this diverse group, including early Quakers, asking such fundamental questions as "Who was/is Jesus? Is the Christ we worship the very same as the historical Jesus who was crucified at Jerusalem?" And being no less diverse than we are, they came up with different answers. (Unhappily, being less tolerant of their diversity than we have learnt to become of ours. each faction tended to insist that their answer was right and all others wrong!).

The distinction between "the history" and "the mystery" is not one of my own glib journalistic inventions but comes from the Familist John Everard in the 1640s, and possibly a little earlier. Everard thought the historical Jesus irrelevant: "Our Christ must be a Christ formed in us". This exaltation of a present mystical Christ over a past historical Jesus was taken up not only by so-called "Ranters" like Joseph Salmon and Abiezer Coppe but by radical Baptists, and was coupled with a questioning, which often became outright rejection, of the view that the bible record was infallible and historical. Thus it was preached among the sectaries of the New Model Army that "the flesh of Christ and the letter of Scripture were the two great idols of Antichrist".

So it is hardly surprising to find these views among early Quakers, who for a time were not as distinct from the Familists, Ranters and radical Baptists as they later became. George Fox himself, and those most close to him, were conspicuously less interested in the Jesus who died at Jerusalem sixteen hundred years earlier and more concerned with what they experienced or perceived as "the inward light of Christ", or "the light of Christ in our conscience". This subjective inwardness of the light, the power, the seed, this absorption of Christ into humanity, was deeply shocking to prevailing Puritanism which experienced Jesus as outward and objective. Combined as it was with early Friends' rejection of absolute biblical authority, demotion if not outright abandonment of atonement doctrine, and a revolutionary restatement of the second coming (it was happening already in human hearts, they said, and was not to be understood as a literal future event), we understand why orthodox or conservative contemporaries found the Quaker view of Jesus shocking, heretical, even atheistic.

It is true that Fox specifically denied that his emphasis on a subjective experience of Christ within meant that Quakers were indifferent to the historical Jesus. When one of his earliest "Children of the Light" associates, Rhys Jones, visited him in Derby jail in 1651 and plainly expressed the view that "there was never any such thing" as the Jesus who died at Jerusalem, Fox distanced himself from a "slander" which he clearly perceived as unnecessarily damaging to the emergent Quaker movement. But throughout the 1650s, and well beyond, theologically orthodox (i.e. Puritan) critics of Quakerism tended to associate the movement with Rhys Jones' radical view rather than Fox's more prudent ambiguities. Thus Thomas Collier, in *A Looking-Glasse for the Quakers* (1657) asserts that Quakers and "Ranters" would have "no Christ but within, no Scripture to be a rule... no heaven or glory but here". Richard Baxter in his *Quaker's Catechism* of the same year claimed that Friends denied "that there is any such person as Jesus Christ, who suffered at Jerusalem". John Bunyan castigated Fox and his sect for preaching that "every man in the world has the spirit of Christ", that the Jesus Christ who was crucified did not atone for the sins of the world, was not resurrected in body, did not ascend above the starry heavens and would not come again in person to judge all nations: was, in fact, quite a different Jesus Christ from the one of the Gospel narratives. The Baptist scholar Matthew Caffyn accepted that Quakers "say that they own him who suffered on Mount Calvary", but charged that they meant only "the Spirit within..., which spirit they say is now within their bodies and flesh".

It would be as foolish to impute to the early Quakers what their critics said they believed as it is to judge the critics from Quaker polemics alone. But as Edward Grubb found he had to recognise in his 1914 Swarthmore Lecture *The Historic and Inward Christ*, the attempts by Fox and Edward Burrough to answer their critics' charges on this point were ambivalent. If they were misunderstood, it was their own ambivalence which was to blame. The Collier-Bunyon view of early Quaker theology is well borne out by much contemporary Quaker literature, particularly that which was circulating before Fox's ascendancy. This literature, and not least the early writings of Fox himself, offers new metaphors for Christ, new insights into the meaning of the word, a Christ who is parently for early Friends more mystery than history.

Some of this "mystery" theology derived from groups like the itself-mysterious Family of Love, which interpreted the bible allegorically, and whose surviving members described themselves in the 1680s as "a sort of refined Quakers". It was most fully developed by Gerrard Winstanley in the 1640s. Winstanley taught that God was Reason: "In the beginning of time the great creator, Reason, made the earth to be a common treasury". Reason was suffused throughout creation: "The whole of creation... is the clothing of God". God himself was not to be understood in a realist sense: "The Father is the universal power that hath spread himself in the whole globe; the Son is the same power drawn into and appearing in one single person". Everyone can become a Son in this sense.

If much of this anticipates Spinoza (who was influenced by Friends in the 1650s after his excommunication by the Jewish synagogue in Amsterdam, and who said that "Moses and the prophets without was nothing to him except he came to know it within", and applied the same understanding to Jesus), and even William Blake ("All deities reside in the human breast"), Winstanley also precedes Fox in his use of the seed metaphor: "Christ lying in the grave, like a corn of wheat buried under the clod of the earth for a time, and Christ rising up from the powers of your flesh, above that corruption and above those clouds, treading the curse under his feet, is to be seen within". To punch the point home, "The outward Christ or the outward God... sometimes proves devils". He who supposes "God is in the heavens above the skies, and so prays to that God which he imagines to be there... worships his own imagination, which is the devil". Indeed, Winstanley tells us he prefers the word Reason to the word God "because I have been held under darkness by that word (God], as I see many people are".

The widespread contemporary perception of early Friends as a sect which demoted the historical Jesus and replaced him by a mystery-Christ within was plainly a principal (if often unacknowledged) reason for their persecution by orthodox Puritans. Calvinist Puritanism, the orthodoxy of the age, was rooted in the double conviction that the scriptures were infallible both as a guide to sound doctrine and as an historical record of the doings and sayings of first century Jesus. By denying biblical infallibility and inventing new metaphors for Jesus as mystery, Quakers seemed to be departing from the very essence of Protestant faith. Indeed, the widespread fear that Quakers were secret papal agents, Jesuits in disguise, which seems so laughable today, is suddenly explicable when we understand it in these terms. For had not Roman Catholicism placed the mystery of elaborate symbolism over the history as plainly related in the bible? Had not its priests made the historical Jesus play second fiddle to the mystery of the "real presence"? The Quakers, it seemed to the Bunyans and Baxters, were doing something similar, and thereby threatening the Reformed faith.

The early Quakers and other radicals who began questioning and downgrading the historicity of the bible paved the way for the Enlightenment (a good Quaker-rooted word!) and for modern biblical criticism. For us today, the historical Jesus has receded further with the passing centuries. Strauss and Schweitzer persuaded us long ago that he is irrecoverable. (When I wrote this in my first draft of this paper for the Quaker Theology Seminar I was reprimanded by our biblical scholars. Strauss and Schweitzer are old hat, I was told, and if I joined the right study group and read the right books I would learn that today's scholars have embarked on a "new quest" for the historical Jesus which reopens the files Schweitzer thought closed. But on diligent enquiry I find that, new quest or old, no-one has yet turned up a single contemporary record, Roman, Greek or Jewish, of the man Jesus. A vast amount has been accomplished in shedding light on the context of early-first-century Jewish and Greek religious thought, but we still have nothing an historian would recognise as a reliable fact about Jesus: not a trace till towards the end of the first century, and then in religious polemics in mythological dress - virgin birth, water into wine, resurrection, ascension - rather than in any historical record. When I put this to my critics they responded: "What do you expect? Why should we imagine we can find any contemporary record of one local trouble-maker among many?" But that is my point exactly. I do not expect it, and if they don't either, then on what basis can they insist that an historical Jesus remains a necessary foundation of our faith?).

But who needs Strauss and Schweitzer when we have the authority of our own Quaker tradition? Long before other Christian denominations, Friends abandoned belief in the Gospel narratives as historical truth, joining Fox's friend Samuel Fisher in the view that the bible is "a bulk of heterogenous writings compiled together by men taking what they could find... and crowding then into a canon". It is "a huge heap of uncertainties". Whatever else may be found there, it is not certainties about the historical Jesus. We can have more confidence in an historical Confucious and Buddha than an historical Jesus.

If the history is uncertain, what of the mystery? The mystery is encoded in the language of poetry and metaphor. Winstanley first, and Fox a few years later, expressed new conceptions of Christ in powerful new metaphors (the seed, inward teacher), or old ones given a new twist (the light, the power, the spirit). Three and a half centuries and innumerable revolutions in thought later, we find ourselves still picking over these metaphors to extract a meaning for our very different times, to discover whether the mystery which replaced the history still speaks to our condition.

Here, though with some trepidation in the face of both his scholarly erudition and his spiritual insight, I want to query what R Melvin Keiser says in his paper *Christ in the Mesh of Metaphor*. Metaphor, he suggests, symbolizes or connects us with "reality". ("Metaphor bears us beyond the words to the reality itself"). The mesh of seed, light, power, way metaphors provides a verbal likeness of a non-verbal reality. I confess I have difficulty imagining what this non-verbal "reality" could be. Melvin Keiser would perhaps say that it is precisely because we find the reality difficult to grasp that we need the metaphors! But I am not clear on what basis we are to assume that there is a non-verbal reality to which metaphor connects us. Just as words can only be defined in terms of other words, can a metaphor do more than connect us with other words? Can we really think ourselves beyond language to some wordless reality?

To put it more plainly, do the metaphors of way, truth and life offer a likeness of a reality rooted (another metaphor!) in the silence (another!) beyond (yet another!) language, or are the words "God" and "Christ" themselves metaphors, words connecting us with other words? I find it hard to grasp them as anything other than the latter. Fox's own wonderfully rich and thrilling mesh of metaphors serves to connect me with another metaphor: for are not "Christ", "Son" and "the living God" themselves metaphors for values which have been historically and culturally developed and made "real" by language?

If, then, the history is irrecoverable and the mystery is not related to an outward "ultimate reality" but to the properties of human language, what is left? Who do we say that Jesus is? Who is the presence in our midst?

What is left is the story, the whole magnificent, inspirational, redemptive story of Jesus as it has come down to us in the "New Testament" and the non-canonical gospels. In the light and power of the story, it is as irrelevant as it is unprovable whether Jesus was as historical as Julius Caesar, as mythological as the wizard Merlin or as re-invented as Shakespeare's Hamlet and Macbeth. Jesus may or may not have lived as the Gospel-writers describe; the mystical Christ may be no more (but no less) than an historically developed concept within one particular human culture which we call Christian; but we do have something real and tangible to grasp, and that is the wonderful story of God and Christ as laid out for us in the ancient writings we call the Bible and in subsequent written tradition (not excluding Winstanley and Fox). All human life is there in this epic story, where God and Christ are the main movers and shakers. The only real Jesus is the Jesus of the stories, the Jesus into whose mouth the so-called "sermon on the mount" is put, just as the only real Hamlet is the Hamlet who pondered the question "to be or not to be", a possible historical dark-ages Hamlet being irrelevant to all but academic antiquarians.

If Hamlet is the main character in Hamlet, symbolising the tension between thought and deed, God is the main character in stories about God, symbolising the moral imperatives and values which, though generated by human culture, we have come to think of as transcending human culture. And the Son, Son of Man as well as Son of God, symbolises the essentially human nature of these "divine" values: "For Mercy has a human heart", says Blake, "Pity a human face, And Love the human form divine, And Peace the human dress". And this Mercy, Pity, Peace and Love "is God", and is also "man, His child and care". So "Where Mercy, Peace and Pity dwell, There God is dwelling too".

Mercy, pity, peace, love, seed, light, life, truth, power, wisdom, spirit, way - all may be metaphors for God and Christ, *but God and Christ are also metaphors for them*. This gives real meaning to "seeking the will of God" and following the "leadings of the Spirit". We surely know that there is no "real presence" at meeting, any more than there is in the Roman Catholic mass. Meeting for worship is not a seance, a contact with the ghost of the historical Jesus. Our sense of the presence of God, of Christ Jesus, is real enough: but it is the *sense*, the *experience*, which is real, not the presence. The two perceptions are very different. If we suppose we are making supernatural contact with the real spirit of a real being, we are in dangerous territory.

If we understand our experience of presence as part of the mesh of metaphor, it can enrich and transform us. So what is the presence in our midst at meeting for worship? Not the white, whispy ghost of an artist's impression, nor the history alone, nor the mystery alone, but the God at the centre of our God-story: the richest metaphor we humans are ever likely to invent.

Awakenings

Text of a talk given to the Quaker Universalist Group conference on "Spiritual Awakenings", 1998

My brief is to talk about my own spiritual awakenings, not to theorise about them. I'll do my best, but to describe experience is also to reflect on it, and to reflect on why the experience is significant and meaningful is to explore and theorise. I know Quakers don't like theorising, but my theory is that they can't avoid it!

I must start by saying that if "awakenings" are to be understood as "spiritual experiences" in the sense of encounters with external spirits or supernatural forces, then this contribution will be mercifully short. I have had no such experiences, and do not believe in them. The peak experiences I will describe may say something about the wholly human spirit, which is the only Holy Spirit I know.

First: I am four years old. My mother has been teaching me my letters by showing me cards. I am learning that each squiggly shape on the card goes with a funny sound - but at this stage I have no understanding that these shapes and sounds relate to words, or anything other than themselves. It's just a noisy, gurgly game to play with my mum.

One morning I look out of the window to see the milk float arrive at our gate. I notice on the side of the float one of those shapes from the cards: M. I make the sound. Then I see that next to it is another shape: I. Then L, then K. I make all the sounds together: M-I-L-K. For the first time, *gloria in excelsis*, I make the connection. The horizons of my little world suddenly expand to infinity. I do not know it, but I have discovered *signs* and *language*. More than sixty years on, I still remember the thrill of that discovery.

Second: I am three or four years older. I can read now. I am taken to the county library and shown the shelves of children's books, with big letters and lots of illustrations. But what really catches my attention and astonishes me is the row on row, shelf on receding shelf, of books for grown-ups: boring books with tiny print *and no pictures*! Again I have awoken to a new world: a world where all the knowledge in the universe appears to be encoded in print in the Ashford Middlesex library. In a delirium of excitement, I vow that I will eat of this tree of knowledge by reading every one of these books, by which I shall surely come to know everything. I also vow that one day I shall write my own boring books with exquisitely tiny print and no pictures: one of the few childhood ambitions I have lived to achieve.

The urge to read as much as possible was further fuelled by my being taught, in our Plymouth Brethren home, that the second coming of Jesus was imminent. It might be a full month or two away, but was to be expected any moment. I remember the alarm I felt that he might come before I could get through the library. (A few years later, when the most interesting awakenings I was experiencing had something to do with my growing realisation that girls were different, I had a similar dread that he might come before I could practise what my hormones were preaching! "Even so, come, Lord Jesus" - but not yet!).

I pass over the every-day awakenings of common experience: the joyous discovery of poetry, music, *fellowship*, the shocked discovery of injustice which swept me first into left-wing politics and then into campaigning broadcast journalism, "afflicting the comfortable and comforting the afflicted". So to my third Great Awakening.

Third: Buying a ruined 17th-century farmhouse in the Yorkshire Dales, I started to research its history, discovering that it had been the home of Quaker pioneers. Delving into the old Quaker records, I rediscovered the richness of religious language: the language of the Bible, of Fox, of the farming families - the Haygarths and Thistlethwaites, Masons, Burtons and Wilkinsons - who had struggled to build Jerusalem in these green and pleasant dales. I awoke, to find I had come home.

To what, then, did I awake? To the thrilling discovery that language is what makes us human; language is the water in which the wholly human spirit swims. And words made flesh in my experience awakened me to the needs of the world, and to our human responsibility when we realise that "no saviour from on high delivers". I leave you to decide whether such awakenings are "spiritual", but they have renewed and refreshed my spirits.

Mysticism and Mystification

*This correspondence began as a private exchange between myself and Jan Arriens,
author of a QUG pamphlet 'The Place of Jesus in Quaker Universalism', following
publication of my QUG pamphlet 'The Faith of a Quaker Humanist'. The letters
were subsequently edited (by both of us) for publication in 'The Friend', February 20
1998*

Dear Jan,

It was generous of you to respond so warmly, if critically, to my QUG
pamphlet. There's a lot we agree on: that religions are human creations, that
- as Blake puts it - "all deities reside in the human breast". And, as Blake
again has it, humanity and divinity are inseparably interfused, which is the
meaning of incarnation.

But you want to make an exception for what you call "mystical experience".
God and faith are human creations, you agree, but mystical experience is not.
It is "beyond human formalisations and formulations", "the fount and origin
of all religion". Where, then, does it come from? Not from God, evidently,
since what transcends humanity can hardly come from a God who lives and
moves and has his being entirely within human language and culture. But if
not from God, then from what? This is where mysticism begins to look to
me like mystification.

You see mystical experience as beyond human language and culture. I see it
as wholly human. You link it to something supernatural, I to the natural.
When Blake was asked where his visions - his mystical experiences - came
from, he tapped his forehead. Yes, he had the keenest sense of the
transcendent - but he knew that the transcendent too belongs to the human
imagination. I do not doubt the reality of such experiences, but I no more
feel the need to attribute them to something supernatural or superhuman
than I do to attribute mental illness to possession by devils.

It seems to me dangerous to lay too much stress on the mystical as the
essence of religious experience. To the truly religious, and surely to the
Quaker, every aspect of life is religious - the humdrum no less than the
ineffable. If "pure religion and undefiled... is to visit the fatherless and
widows in their affliction", to buy a copy of *Big Issue* from a homeless
youngster (and, far better, to agitate for ending the causes of homelessness)

is a more essentially religious experience than a familiar sense of the unity of all things or a mystical sense of contact with some undefined and indefinable Beyond.

In friendship, David

Dear David

If all religion, including mystical experience, is wholly human, what is worship? I remember worshipping with you at Brigflatts and wondering precisely what meeting for worship meant to a humanist. And this brings me to a potentially major divide. This is that you say nothing in your booklet about the *shared* silence. I agree about "finding worth", and not worshipping some-thing, but for me the essence of the Quaker silence is the extra dimension brought by the corporate element ("where two or three are gathered in my name...").

I remember the first time I went to Quaker meeting, just to see what it was like. What I had not bargained for was the group dimension. The meeting was quite different from a group meditation, in which one concentrates on one's mantra or breathing. Instead I found myself effortlessly swept up in something greater - what I now know as a "gathered meeting". I was astonished and exhilarated, and it is this, above all, that has kept me coming to meeting for worship (against all expectations!).

Now you do not mention any corporate dimension, except to say that meeting is a valuable hour "in the company of Friends". I really would be most interested to know what the "gathered" meeting means to you. Does the company of Friends simply supply a container, a kind of stiffening, or is your reaction to meeting as I have tried to describe?

Yours in Friendship, Jan

Dear Jan

You may well be right to suggest that I treat worship too individualistically in my booklet. I was trying to answer the question "What does a Quaker humanist do in meeting for worship?", where a personal answer seemed appropriate. But I agree that it is a corporate and not an individualistic activity. For me it is an act of collective solidarity with the tradition, an undogmatic way of affirming and celebrating the values which the tradition exemplifies. So in worshipping God "after the manner of Quakers", I join with Friends in affirming the "mercy, pity, peace and love" which, says Blake (again) "is God", and at the same time "is man" (or humanity).

You will not be surprised to know that I do not attribute any mystical significance to meeting for worship! I certainly don't experience it as some kind of seance with the risen Christ or encounter with the supernatural. I am not myself much at home with current Quaker-speak, with its "gathered meetings" and "centring down". I must also confess that, while I treasure the memory of wonderful meetings empowered by the spirit (the wholly human spirit), it is rare that the experience matches the intensity of listening to great music (or singing in a choir), enjoying an inspired performance of Shakespeare, or sitting in a darkened cinema to watch *Priest* or *Wilde* or *Shine*. Our Sunday morning meetings are invaluable, but I believe it is what we choose to do with the remaining 167 hours of the week which determines whether we are "in the life".

In friendship, David

Dear David,

You write that mystical experiences do not need a God (agree) or supernatural power to validate them (disagree). It is not even a matter of validation, but of encounter; it is of the essence of the experience.

If we deny any such dimension or realm of consciousness, or call it what we will, and bring everything back to the human level, it seems to me that morality and the things we most believe in life are left hanging by their bootstraps. What then is the rationale for compassion, mercy or pity? If there is nothing higher, these are no more than manifestations of evolutionary, survival-based drives. This seems to me unutterably bleak.

I have to say that to me all the finest qualities to which you allude only make sense if placed in a wider, transcendent frame of reference. If you could explain what a humanist bases morality on, I'd be genuinely grateful.

Yours in Friendship, Jan

Dear Jan

I honestly don't understand the notion that morality must have some supernatural authority or reference point, without which it is "left hanging by its bootstraps". Why is there a problem in recognising that morality, like the law, is human-made, reflecting the experience and (of course fallible) collective wisdom of human communities? Isn't that just a plain statement of how things are, even if we might feel more secure in having our morality validated by supernatural authority?

If we treat a neighbour kindly, we do not do so because God or some unnamed mystical superhuman power tells us to. We do it because we humans have imagination, and imagination enables us to put ourselves in the place of others, and putting ourselves in the place of others creates sympathy, and sympathy prompts us to do as we would be done by. I know you do wonderful work writing to prisoners on America's Death Row. Do you do it in obedience to some external command or super-human rule-book, or because you have a keen imaginative sympathy with those to whom you write? Would you stop writing if you ceased to believe that your actions were supernaturally validated? If loving our enemies is right, it is surely not right just because Jesus said so. Do we not believe, *have we not chosen to believe*, that it would be right even if Jesus had never said any such thing?

You ask what a humanist bases morality on. Well, this humanist finds no basis beyond human imaginative sympathy, human negotiation, human consensus (which this *Quaker* humanist would want to express in the religious language of the Quaker tradition). It involves a humble recognition that morality is not absolute: it changes with historical circumstances, evolves differently in different cultures, and is embodied in constantly-changing human language. It is *our* responsibility! What I really would find "unutterably bleak" is the idea that what you call "the rationale for compassion, mercy or pity" is some mystical superhuman agency. Not only bleak but dangerous, leading well-intentioned men and women, as it all-too-often does, to claim divine authority for their all-too-human understandings. We know all too well where that can lead.

I don't ask you to agree, only to reflect on an approach which tries to give a contemporary twist to a Quakerism born within a seventeenth-century world view. You have made me reflect on your own strand of Quaker universalism, and I am deeply grateful.

In friendship, David

What on Earth is Religious Humanism?

*An address to a conference on religious humanism organised by the Sea of Faith
Network in September 2000. The text was published in SOF magazine, January
2001.*

Our theme is "religious humanism". So - what on Earth is it? Is it any
more than an historical oddity, embedded in the dry bones of 19th-
century "ethical societies", "religions of humanity" and socialist
Sunday schools? Is it still alive and well in postmodernity, and if so, where is
it hiding? Can it speak to our 21st-century condition? What is religious
about it? What is humanist about it? And what can we do with it?

For a start, why are we talking about it now? The pragmatic answer is that
this conference is organised by Sea of Faith, and "religious humanism" is one
of the ways Sea of Faith has of describing its distinctive outlook. From its
foundation in the 1980s, the Sea of Faith Network formulated its aims and
objects as the exploration and promotion of "religious faith as a human
creation". That's religious humanism in a nutshell. At the Network's 1991
annual conference, Don Cupitt, debating with the Rationalist Nicolas
Walter, argued that "the various Enlightenment, liberal and Marxist versions
of humanism have broken down no less dramatically than traditional
religious belief". But the business of making meaning, of re-imagining
ourselves, our values, our world, has to go on. In the past, it went on
communally and unconsciously, "and the result [said Cupitt] was what we
call religion". But now we are conscious of what we are up to, and "because
we do it consciously, it will be a sort of humanism, but because we know we
still need communal myths and rituals, it will also be religion. We shall be
religious humanists, making believe."

Two years later, in 1993, the Anglican priest Anthony Freeman published a
book with a splendidly Quakerish title, *God in Us*, which he subtitled "The
Case for Christian Humanism". I have long suspected that what really
scandalised the bishops and led them to cry "Crucify him! Crucify him!" and
remove him from his parish was not Anthony's blunt refusal to pretend that
he believed in a celestial Big Brother but his open use of the dreaded H-
word. Humanism, to the noble army of mitres, is the antithesis of religion.
Christian humanism is to them the ultimate oxymoron. The H-word on the
title-page of a book by a licensed priest has, to Church fathers, much the

same effect as the F-word would have on the masthead of the Mothers' Union journal.

Two years after the Freeman affair, in 1995, *Sea of Faith* magazine surveyed the Network membership and found that "religious humanist" or "Christian humanist" was the most popular label members chose to apply to themselves, ahead of such alternatives as "nonrealist" and "radical Christian". Some preferred variants such as "Eco-Humanist", "Quaker Humanist", and just plain non-adjectival "Humanist". Virtually every year since then, Don Cupitt has been telling SoF conferences that "We urgently need... a new this-worldly and democratic religious humanism". At this year's conference he defined this new-style, this-worldly religious humanism as "our human way of first imagining new values and a better world, and then actually working to bring them about".

The same conference also took religious humanism out of the narrow confines of western Christian culture by examining, with the radical Buddhist writer Stephen Batchelor, what a desupernaturalised Buddhist humanism might look like. The Network is also building bridges with the two Jewish humanist networks - Reconstruction Judaism and Humanistic Judaism - which have begun to make an impact on Jewish life in the last thirty years, particularly in the United States. Thus "religious humanism" has progressively shed its old, narrow, bloodless, filleted, half-this-half-that image and fought its way back onto a field from which the oddly combined forces of bishops, rabbis, gurus and rationalists had thought they had driven it.

Having said that, I have to admit that by no means all Sea of Faith members, or Quaker Universalists like myself, share the enthusiasm which some of us have for "religious humanism" as a description of our "position". The main reason for this in SoF is resistance to the idea that the Network *has* anything resembling an *ideology*: some members take the commitment to "religious faith as a human creation" as loosely and poetically as they take the creeds, liturgies and other forms of God-talk: it's just a picturesque form of words, they seem to suggest, not to be taken literally or seriously. For them, the Network is not primarily an organisation promoting the understanding that religion and its gods are wholly human creations, but an open forum for exploration of religious ideas in general and doctrinal doubts in particular, un-anchored by any commitment to anything. This is a potential fault-line which may one day open up and swallow us whole: the Network as open forum full stop, or the Network as open forum promoting a particular view of religion - the view that, like music, politics, football and summer pudding, religion is a human creation. My own view is simple. If we go down the open-forum-full-stop road and back away from our commitment to promote the understanding that religious faith is a wholly human creation without even a sliver of extra-terrestrial input, we may end up with the need to invent a new network to explore and promote religious faith as a human creation! But this is not the place to pursue apocalyptic Network politics!

There are other reasons why "religious humanism" as a term descriptive of SoF's position is embraced with only modified rapture by some members. At the last survey, fractionally over half of the Network's membership had no church, Quaker-meeting or other institutional religious allegiance whatever, and fractionally under half did, either as professionals (our famous "godless vicars" tendency), or as committed but questioning church-goers, or just hanging on by the skin of their clenched teeth. In both tendencies there are those who find reason to avoid the term "religious humanism". In the church tendency there are those who dislike the baggage which the word "humanism" brings with it: the old association with militant atheism, strident secularism, anti-clericalism, and a somewhat bloodless high-mindedness devoid of the warmth, protection and rich community spirit which churches, chapels, meetinghouses, synagogues and temples have aimed at providing.

In the non-church tendency, on the other hand, it is the baggage which comes with the word "religious" which is the problem: baggage to do with dogmatism, authoritarianism, holy war, patriarchy, dressing up in silly clothes, vicars' voices, bad reproductions of sentimental paintings of earnest men in robes and langorous women in very little, "washed in the blood" choruses, misty mysticisms, life after death, gaseous spiritualities and money-spinning new age quackery.

So for some the word "religious" is ok, "humanism" not: for others, "religious" is the dodgy word, "humanism" the ok one. For these, the hyper-sensitively baggage-conscious on both sides, "religious humanism" doesn't so much build bridges as erect road-blocks.

And there's another reason why "religious humanism" has yet to convince everyone that it's the right label for our particular bottle. It's called history. "Religious humanism" has meant different things in different times and different places. What it would have meant to Erasmus, or Winstanley, or Spinoza, had they heard the term, would not be what it means to us. We tend to see modern religious humanism as a 19th century phenomenon, emerging from such developments as the growth of Unitarianism (which reduced the three persons of the divinity into one, and then began to wonder whether that wasn't one too many), and, philosophically, from Ludwig Feuerbach's revolutionary book, translated by George Eliot as *The Essence of Christianity*, which argued that God had been imagined into being by humanity, not the other way round. For a while this kind of religious humanism flourished in organisations like August Comte's Church of Humanity, where deity was replaced by Man, the Pope by August Comte, and church ritual by naff ceremonies which retained priestly vestments, smells and flowery language but struggled, rather like Basil Fawlty and the war, to avoid any mention of God.

Comte's Religion of Humanity was, as Churchill remarked of a minor politician named Bossom, neither one thing nor the other, and something of the same instability marked the Unitarian strand of religious humanism. Samuel Taylor Coleridge, himself a former Unitarian lay-preacher, noted this instability as early as 1812, when he wrote that a Unitarian is "a man who has passed from orthodoxy to the loosest Arminianism and thence to Arianism, and thence to direct Humanism". The final step in this downward escalator, said Coleridge, is "to fall off into the hopeless abyss of atheism". Coleridge was right to predict that the centre of *this kind* of religious humanism would not hold. Nicolas Walter writes entertainingly, though you may think somewhat cruelly if you happen to be a Unitarian, of the way in which American Unitarianism in particular became consumed by the struggle between "God-men" and "No-God-men" (Unitarian women were presumably making the tea at the time): "There was a danger of schism...but first the Humanists began to leave, and then the God-men began to adopt Humanism as well".

This inherent instability was seen in the decline during the 20th century of the ethical societies which had looked so promising in the 19th. South Place, itself Unitarian in origin, which had proclaimed as one of its objectives the "cultivation of a rational religious sentiment", found that facing both ways only produced a chronic crick in the neck. Religious members tended to slip back into the churches and those who couldn't work out what a rational religious sentiment might look like when the lights were switched on turned the Society into a non-religious or anti-religious humanist body with nothing stronger than nostalgia to connect it to religious humanism. The story was much the same in other once religious-humanist organisations.

No doubt individual psychologies played a major part in all this. Some members were reluctant to abandon the psychological and sociological support of their religious background, while others found it a psychological and sociological necessity to break with their religious past. That was the inherent instability. One result was that some big names who still called themselves religious humanists, like Julian Huxley and Albert Einstein, were wholly cut off from the culture of religion, while others who also owned the religious humanist label, like Albert Schweitzer, Paul Tillich and Martin Buber, made no connection whatever with the wider humanist movement.

So that's another reason, I suspect, why some Sea of Faith members have been a bit leary about waving the "religious humanism" flag. It has a faded look about it, like an old trade union banner which has seen one too many demos. It's a bit threadbare in places, and the colours have faded. Along with Horlicks and the BBC Third Programme, it belongs to a warmly-remembered past, but it doesn't seem cool these days to wave it about.

Well, I want to say that I'm not interested in trying to revive 19th and early 20th-century religious humanism. My hope is that we can start a process which builds *a radical new religious humanism fit for the 21st century*. I would be running far beyond my abilities if I were to try to offer a detailed blueprint of the radical religious humanism I have in mind. But I can toss out some headline-thoughts which others may follow up. First, some negative ones: ideas of what radical religious humanism is *not*, rather than what it might be.

First, it is *not* a half-way house between religion and humanism, a refuge for those who simply can't make up their minds. Radical religious humanism must be more than a safe house for those who want to have their theistic cake and eat it. It may provide for some a useful staging-post in a personal journey from one kind of commitment to another, but if that is all it is, it's no big deal.

Secondly, it's *not* a new church or a new religion, not even an embryonic one. That's one of the routes they tried in the 19th century, and it got them nowhere. Some religious humanists will want to express their humanism within an existing religious tradition, others will want to separate themselves from traditional religious institutions. Some will want to devise non-theistic liturgies, some will be happy with liturgies in traditional God-language taken with lashings of metaphor and poetic licence, some won't want any liturgies or rituals at all, thank you very much. Radical religious humanists will remain a diverse lot, but they won't be creating yet another denomination, with yet more appeals for the roof fund and yet another clerical caste.

Thirdly, it's *not* the binary opposite of secular humanism. Radical religious humanism is wholly secular in the root-meaning of the word: it is of this world and for this age, the only world we can know and the only age of which we can have any direct experience. As the title of a Quaker Universalist pamphlet puts it, "There is another world, but it is this one". Radical religious humanism, having taken leave of God for God's sake, has taken leave of any notion of an after-life, of the supernatural, of any mystical realm beyond the bounds of our universe. Radical religious humanists are as much aware as any secular, rationalist or scientific humanist that we are on our own, "no Saviour from on high delivers", and whatever gods and godesses, spirits and demons, angels and devils we share our lives with, they are of our own making, imagined into being by human communities, within human culture.

So what *is* religious about modern religious humanism? Let me take you back to that 1991 debate between Don Cupitt and Nicolas Walter. This is Nicolas, in full flow:

"We [that is *non-religious* humanists] reject the whole of religion, not just the difficult bits. We reject the whole of the Bible, not just the supernatural bits. We reject Jesus the man just as much as Jesus the God. We reject the doctrines of all the scriptures, and the deeds of all the churches. We see religion not as a necessary stage in the evolution of humanity, but as a long mistake - rather as Communism and Fascism were short mistakes. We see the shift from religion to non-religion as a process not of progressive revelation of changing truths but of progressive realisation of changing lies. We see not so much the loss of faith as the recovery of sanity. Whether we prefer a Hegelian or Marxist or Darwinian or Freudian or some other interpretation of religion, we think not just that it is wrong now but that it was always wrong".

Religion - humanity's long mistake? The immense, age-long accumulation of religious writing, music, art, dance, architecture; the infinitely complex system of imaginative symbols by which human beings explored their own humanity in a mysterious, awesome, wonderful world; the long search for values which transcend the needs and desires of individual egos; the myths and legends, stories, songs, parables, poems, proverbs, visions, exhortations of the Hebrew Bible, the Mahabharata, Rumi and Hafiz, native Americans and native Australians, John Donne, William Blake, Gerard Manley Hopkins, T S Eliott, R S Thomas, Bach's music, Mozart's masses, Mahler's Resurrection - *one long mistake?*

I don't think so. And if that's where non-religious humanism stands, it's just too thin and undernourished for me: anorexic humanism. For a humanism to cut itself off from some of the crowning achievements of wholly human culture seems to me both tragic and absurd. It's like drinking non-alcoholic wine, or making love without taking your clothes off: nice up to a point, but there's definitely something missing. So long as mainstream humanism persists in cutting itself off from mainstream humanity in this way, for just so long will it remain a minority interest.

Radical religious humanism does *not* take the view that humanity's religious heritage is a long mistake. It does *not* suppose that homo sapiens has just been liberated from a darkness which lasted from the year dot to the dawn of the Rationalist Press Association.

Radical religious humanism is a secular humanism, a rational humanism, an ethical humanism which feels free to draw on, to feast on, the best of our long, complex, diverse heritage of religious expression. It knows all too well the madness, brutality, hypocrisy and repressiveness of religion at its worst, as indeed of humanity itself at its most inhumane. But this does not blind it to the glories it glimpses of religious inspiration at its best. There are bad people, but we are not anti-people; bad politics, but we are not anti-politics; bad art, but we are not philistine; bad science, but we are not anti-scientific. And there is wretched religion, but that is no good reason for basing one's entire life-stance on an undiscriminating war on all religious expression.

Radical religious humanism is a humanism which makes free with the resources of religion in its richly diverse forms, as with the resources of the whole of human culture. We know that we made it all, so we can unmake it and remake it. If we call on God to help us, we know we are using a powerful figure of speech. If we seek God's will, we know that we are simply looking for the best course, in the best interest of all. If we pray, we know we are talking to ourselves - and who doesn't do that, and gain benefit from it? If we ask forgiveness, and for the strength to follow the light of our conscience, we know we are expressing our desire to be better people. If we say we are working for the republic of heaven (even if we can't get out of the habit of calling it the Kingdom), we know we are talking about taking action to make the world a better place for the whole of humankind.

The binary opposition is not between religion and humanism. Nor, as I have said, is it between secular humanism and religious humanism. There are diferences, of course - Nicolas Walter spelt them out - between religious and non-religious or anti-religious humanism. But I believe these differences, or at least the tensions arising from them, are diminishing. Writing in 1997, six years after his SoF debate with Don Cupitt, Nicolas Walter acknowledged that "many... see themselves as both humanist and religious... The progressive elements in the Christian churches in Britain who have been abandoning theism and joining in the Sea of Faith movement call their position 'Christian Humanism'... It is wrong to call these positions 'contradictions in terms' or to call their adherents hypocrites". In the last three years of his life, Nicolas included *Sea of Faith* magazine among the humanist journals he wrote for, and today you'll find Sea of Faith by-lines in the RPA's *New Humanist*, and the British Humanist Association glitterati on SoF platforms and in SoF anthologies. We have come to recognise that we have a lot in common.

Modern radical religious humanism is not the last relic of Victorian doubt, or progressive Christianity's last desperate kick. It is something new. It rationalises religion and enriches humanism. It dissolves the old differences between the sacred and the secular, the human and the divine, the natural and the supernatural. It does not deify humanity, but it understands that our values are human values, and could be no other. It offers change, growth, renewal. It's for those who can face a life on the ocean wave rather than those who prefer a safe harbour. It's for the seeker rather than the finder, for those who would make their own meaning and purpose rather than buy them off the peg. It demands faith, hope, charity, determination - and a well-developed sense of humour.

Part Two

History

Winstanley and Friends

This essay combines an article written for "Friends Quarterly", April 2000, and a paper delivered to the Conference of Quaker Historians at Earlham College, Richmond, Indiana, USA, in June 2000. It also draws on an article in "Political Theology", May 2001

Was Gerrard Winstanley a Quaker? Did he have any direct connection with Quakers? Did George Fox read his books and pamphlets, and was he influenced by them? These questions - the first two, at least - were asked in the seventeenth century, and have been asked again by historians and scholars in the twentieth. Those of us who have been inspired by Winstanley's radicalism have hoped that the piecemeal scraps of documented information will indeed prove him "one of us": those who distrust his politics, and particularly his communism, will breathe a sigh of relief if it can be shown that True Levelling and Quakers never did more than flirt with each other, and certainly never consummated their coy relationship. This article is an attempt to set out the known facts, and to summarise the conclusions I have reached while researching my book, *Gerrard Winstanley and the republic of heaven.*

Winstanley was born in Wigan, Lancashire, in 1609. He was probably educated at Wigan grammar school, as his writing is fluent if not particularly scholarly, and he made use of the occasional Latin tag. In or around 1630 he travelled south to London to be apprenticed to a merchant tailor, Sarah Gates, who was probably a kinswoman. She was the widow of a former puritan minister turned cloth merchant and possessed a well-stocked theological library in her home, where Winstanley probably lodged. In 1637 he became a freeman of the Merchant Tailors Company and in 1640 married Susan King, daughter of a small landowner in Cobham, Surrey. In 1643, with the country plunged into civil war, his cloth business failed. "I was beaten out both of estate and trade," he wrote, "and forced... to live a country life". He seems to have been employed by his father-in-law as a grazier and cowherd in Cobham.

The great swirl of political and religious dissent soon pulled him into its vortex. From having been brought up "a strict goer to church... and hearer of sermons", he turned to "the ordinance of dipping" (baptism), at a time when the more radical Baptist congregations were denouncing all forms of church establishment and providing a stream of recruits to the Leveller movement and the New Model Army. (The same stream would later be diverted into Quakerism). But Winstanley preferred the pen to the sword. Early in 1648 he delivered to a notoriously radical-sectarian printer, Giles Calvert, who had a printing shop in the crowded alleys behind the old pre-fire St Paul's cathedral, the manuscript of the first of three pamphlets he would publish that year. Another seventeen would follow within four years, mostly published by Calvert, who was printer to the Levellers and, a few years later, to the Quakers.

The Mysterie of God was an extraordinary literary debut. It is probably the first theological work in the English language to argue what became known as the "universalist" doctrine that everyone, however sinful, would be saved. The prevailing Calvinist orthodoxy preached that the fate of all was divinely preordained, the few to salvation, the many to damnation. Even those like the General Baptists who denied predestination accepted that eternal damnation was the lot of the unrepentant sinner. Winstanley's sweeping universalism had radical political as well as heretical theological implications: puritanism tended to identify the "better sort", the successful and wealthy, with the elect, and the "baser sort", the poor, with the damned. The great and the good were one, as were the small and the bad. Universalism clearly tended to blur if not altogether erase the distinction between the great unwashed and those who had been washed in the blood of the Lamb. It was an alarmingly levelling doctrine.

But Winstanley was not content to argue that the poor would be saved. In *The Mysterie of God* and the two pamphlets which followed, he teaches that it is the poor who are to be God's *agents* in bringing about the kingdom of heaven on earth. When he dares to connect the poor with the radical sectaries, the subversive and revolutionary potential of his doctrine is clear, to priest and magistrate alike.

In his next two pamphlets Winstanley presses the point with a daringly metaphorical interpretation of Biblical scripture. The devil is not a person but the embodiment of selfishness and self-seeking. God is Reason, or seflessness, or community. Christ is not "a man [who] lived and died long ago at Jerusalem" but "the power of the spirit within you". God is not to be looked for "in a place of glory beyond the sun, but within yourself... He that looks for a God outside himself... worships he knows not what, but is... deceived by the imagination of his own heart". Winstanley shared the millenarian expectations of his contemporaries, but the Christ who would come again would be a spirit "rising in despised sons and daughters", an "indwelling power of reason", a "sea of truth" which would wash away corruption and ensure that the lowly and meek inherited the earth.

Moreover, the coming "saints' paradise" was to be built not on clerical book-learning and authority but on direct experience, "experimental knowledge of Christ", "a teacher within". Years before George Fox would say much the same, in almost identical words. Winstanley writes: "What I hear another man speak is nothing to me until I find the same experience in myself. The testimony of others is known to be true by the testimony of the same experience within myself". And again, like Fox, he applied this to the books of the Bible no less than to those of his contemporaries.

But Winstanley was no armchair theoretician, content to sit back and wait for Christ to rise in sons and daughters. Early in 1649 he had a vision, much as Fox was to have at Pendle three years later. In his vision, or "trance", Winstanley was instructed: "Work together. Eat bread together. Declare this all abroad... I the Lord have spoke it". Winstanley interpreted this as a call to action, and on April 1, with a small band of fellow-Diggers, he took possession of some common land at St George's Hill, near Walton-on-Thames, and established a community to till the ground in common, sharing labour and produce. One of his companions, William Everard, reportedly predicted that they would be thousands-strong within ten days. In fact, some fifty men with their families joined them, and over the next twelve months perhaps thirty similar communes came into being, albeit tentatively and briefly, throughout south-east England.

Winstanley's community was immediately attacked by mobs led by those who claimed exclusive proprietary rights to the commons. Leadership of the mob was quickly assumed by the local parson, John Platt, a puritan minister and landlord who objected in both capacities to the actions of those who were now calling themselves "True Levellers". Crops were dug up, shelters pulled down and burnt, and women and children physically assaulted. The winter of 1649, following a disastrous harvest and seven years of crippling warfare, was one of hunger and hardship nation-wide. For Winstanley and his comrades it was a grim struggle to survive, made no easier when a group of Ranters attempted to join, preaching community of women as well as land, and urging violent resistance to the mobs.

A stream of pamphlets from Winstanley's pen denounced parson Platt and his corrupt church, the landlords and their corrupting wealth, and the Ranters and their corrupting influence. He insisted that violence could not be met with violence: God (or Reason) would not rely on "carnal weapons". The Digger's war was a "Lamb's War" against the dragon of property, the principle of selfishness which was the devil incarnate. Winstanley's arguments for making the earth a "common treasury", for turning republican England (Charles I had just been executed) into a republic of heaven [1], are formulated in a total of twenty pamphlets and books, which output is surely among the most lucid and inspirational in England's rich tradition of polemical literature. As Michael Foot writes in his Foreword to my book, "If there were such a thing as a sacred canon of radical English literature, Winstanley's works would be there, not far behind those of Milton, Byron, Shelley, Hazlitt and William Morris". And none of these wrote under such conditions of persecution and destitution as Winstanley endured in the first year of the English, Scottish, Welsh and Irish republic.

But Christ did not rise in sons and daughters, even with the assistance of the Diggers' spades and Winstanley's eloquent pen. Twelve months after the experiment began it was ended with the brutal sacking of the community and the forced dispersal of the dwindling band of comrades. The satellite communes quickly collapsed in turn. Winstanley, who had taught the evils of wage labour, had to turn to wage labour himself to keep himself and his longsuffering wife alive. He wrote one more major work, *The Law of Freedom*, published early in 1652. It is a detailed blueprint for a communist society, and it is addressed to Oliver Cromwell. "Now I have set the candle at your door", he writes, "for you have power in your hand... to act for common freedom if you will; I have no power". Winstanley has not entirely given up hope that "the Lord", understood as a benevolent cosmos, will signal the start of the long-awaited millennial reign; but he now looks to state power to kick-start Christ's rising, where a year or two earlier he had seen state and church together as the twin-headed dragon that would be overcome by the lamb.

The Law of Freedom is an astonishing work, on the basis of which Winstanley would subsequently be labelled a proto-Marxist (though it has been suggested that Marx might more aptly be called a neo-Winstanleyite). Some have seen in the short four years separating *The Mysterie of God* in 1648 from *The Law of Freedom* in 1652 an abandonment of mystical theology for secular politics, but it is plain to me that the politics are already embedded in the first pamphlet and the radical theology remains the core of the last. Politics and religion, the secular and the sacred, were one to Winstanley, as they were to Fox and early Friends, whose new Quaker movement began to achieve lift-off just as True Levelling crash-landed.

Twenty-four years after *The Law of Freedom*, and two years after Winstanley's death, the Dean of Durham, Thomas Comber, published a book, *Christianity no Enthusiasm*, claiming that the Quakers "derived their ideas from the communist writer Gerrard Winstanley", which in his view made "repression of Quakerism... not only a service to God, but a preservation of every man and his property". Although the alleged connection seems not to have been closely pursued at the time (perhaps because by the 1670s the widely-recognised attachment of respectable Friends to private enterprise was enough to give the lie to Comber's crude smear), it was taken up again when Winstanley was rediscovered by nineteenth-century Marxists. Eduard Bernstein in 1895, G P Gooch in 1896 and Lewis Berens in 1906 all claimed that either Winstanley became a Quaker or that the Quakers derived much of their theology from Winstanley. The respectable Quaker historians Rufus M Jones and William C Braithwaite thought the connection doubtful, suggesting that Winstanley and Fox seem, in Braithwaite's words, to be "independent products of the peculiar social and spiritual climate of the age". David Petegorsky's *Left-Wing Democracy in the English Civil War: a Study of the Social Philosophy of Gerrard Winstanley and the Digger Movement*, 1940, was more emphatic, saying "there is no evidence whatever" for any contact between Winstanley and Friends, and this was the view of George Sabine, who published his monumental *Works of Gerrard Winstanley* the following year - though Sabine recognised the "close similarity of religious experience" in Winstanley and Fox. Richard T Vann charted what he saw as Winstanley's journey "from radicalism to Quakerism" in *Journal of Friends Historical Society* Vol 49 (1959-61), but was almost alone among Quaker scholars in searching out the documentation.

There matters stood till the late 1970s when historian Barry Reay unearthed in the Friends House archive a letter sent in August 1654 by Edward Burrough in London to Margaret Fell at Swarthmoor. Burrough and Francis Howgill had been dispatched to the capital by Fox as Quaker missionaries, and Burrough reported that "Wilstandley says he believes we are sent to perfect that work which fell in their hands. He hath been with us". There can be no doubt that the sorely mutilated "Wilstandley" is our man; that he had "been with" Friends, which probably means he had attended their first

London meetings; that he saw the new religion from the north as a continuation of his own work; and that Burrough (the most politically radical of early Friends) was not unsympathetic.

It would be very interesting indeed to have sight of whatever reply Margaret Fell may have made. Quakerism had established its headquarters in a gentry house, under the patronage and matronage of a family which had greatly benefited in wealth and influence from their Cromwellian politics and entrepreneurial adventures. The Fells can hardly have been unaware that "the work" associated with Winstanley was a levelling work, a communist work, dedicated to the overthrow of private property and its replacement by common ownership, under the power of an indwelling God who was more sweet reason than lord of lord protectors. It seems not unlikely to me that Margaret Fell and George Fox discouraged further contacts with so notorious an agitator. Certainly we hear no more of "Wilstandley" from Burrough, Howgill, and the growing band of London Friends.

Not, at least, for many years. But 22 years later we find (or Richard T Vann found, and recorded in the article I have cited) Winstanley's burial record. It is not in any parish register but in that of Westminster Monthly Meeting, which records the burial at Long Acre of Gerrard Winstanley, corn chandler, of St Giles in the Field. It has been suggested that Winstanley's widow, Elizabeth (he had remarried after Susan's death) persuaded Friends to give him a Quaker funeral in honour of his radical past, but this is surely far-fetched. A communist past was not something a widow was likely to want to honour in the reactionary 1670s, and Friends were most unlikely to bury any but their own. It seems clear that some time before he died Gerrard Winstanley became a Quaker. It may be that Elizabeth herself had Quaker connections, for when she remarried in 1681 it was to a Quaker, and the deaths of the three children of Gerrard and Elizabeth are all recorded in the Quaker registers.

But if we can now confidently claim Winstanley as a Friend at the last, we can do so only by opening up another mystery. Other researchers, led by the Canadian scholar James Alsop, have discovered that shortly after his doomed courtship of Friends in 1654, Winstanley took possession of his father-in-law's Surrey estate and began to live the life of a country gentleman. By 1659 "Mr Winstanley" was a waywarden in the parish of Cobham, by 1660, as England reverted to monarchy, he was an overseer, by 1668 a churchwarden, and by 1671 a chief constable - in which capacity he presumably had responsibility for prosecuting Quakers and other dissenters under the Clarendon Code! So it seems that the young radical, forsaken by Reason in his attempt to create a communist republic of heaven, cold-shouldered by Quakers, and then tempted by comfort, security and respectability, had followed the familiar road from radicalism to reaction, before a death-bed repentance brought him back to his radical roots. Christ could yet rise in sons and daughters, even if the republic of heaven was to be a republic not of this world.

In my book I have argued that Winstanley's political and theological trajectory is less baffling once we begin to understand the huge changes in the context within which this all happened. Winstanley changed, certainly, but so did the political and religious world he inhabited. And so too did Quakerism. In 1649 it was distinctly possible to believe that the revolution then in full swing might lead to the extinction of "kingly power", including the rule of wealth and property. The Quaker movement of the 1650s was in part a response to the failure of that revolution to materialise, with a consequent tendency to internalise and spiritualise the republic of heaven as "within" and mystical rather than "without" and this-worldly. The counter-revolution and restoration of monarchy in 1660 put an end to any remaining hopes that the new Jerusalem might be built in England's green and pleasant land. And by the 1670s, their militant republicanism and identification with the "Good Old Cause" conveniently forgotten, Friends were well down the road of respectability, with a reputation for shrewd but honest business dealings, drab clothing and fearsome consciences: "the harmless people of God called Quakers". In truth, the final journey Winstanley made from gentleman to Quaker is not as long as it seems. Friends met him half way.

But if we now know beyond reasonable doubt that Winstanley *did* have contact with Friends in the 1650s and *did* join Westminster Friends in the 1670s, we still lack direct evidence to help us resolve the remaining conundrum: did Winstanley's pre-communist pamphlets influence Fox and early Friends, as the hostile priest Comber alleged? Were the similarities in their works coincidental, attributable to "the spirit of the age", or did Fox read Winstanley and derive some of his inspiration from the older man?

George Fox was some fourteen years younger than Winstanley, born of parents with spectacularly pious pedigrees. He left his Midlands home in 1643, the second year of the civil war, the year Winstanley's cloth business was ruined, and sampled London (where he too had a kinsman). By 1646, his *Journal* tells us, he understood that the university-educated ministry of "hireling priests" was a hindrance to true religion, so he "looked more after the dissenting people", only to find that the separatist preachers could not speak to his condition. What he knew, he knew "experimentally". In 1647 he met up with radical Baptists - "shattered Baptists" he calls them - where he apparently recruited his first followers. As the *Journal* tells it, Fox seems to have been curiously oblivious of the civil discord all around him till, jailed for blasphemy, he was visited in 1651 by a recruiting party for the New Model Army. The recruiting party seems to have regarded his radical dissent as eminent qualification for a commission - which, as he tells us in the *Journal*, he refused. Released later that year, he began his journeyings through the north which would culminate in his meeting the Westmorland Seekers in 1652 and the emergence of an organised Quaker movement.

Thus Winstanley's and Fox's radical religio-political ideologies were formed and framed by the revolutionary convulsions of the 1640s, which saw the established church lose its historic power, the Lords their hereditary seats, and the king his head. There is a critical difference between Winstanley's and Fox's account of these tumultuous times: Winstanley's was written *as the revolution progressed*, every one of his works reflecting a new twist and turn in the power struggle on earth and its cosmic projection in heaven; while Fox's account was dictated and edited-together many years later, when it was no longer politic to foreground the political dimension, which in Fox's mind had by then become almost wholly subsumed in the religious and spiritual. But these very different lenses on the events of the forties cannot disguise the similarities of experience - that which each man "knew experimentally". Both had stopped being a "goer to church", had explored dissent, had been with the radical Baptists, had mixed with Seekers, had tangled with Ranters and with the law, and had found their liberation in an experience of what they believed to be unmediated communion with a God who for the one was sweet Reason "rising in sons and daughters" and for the other was the light of conscience in every man and woman.

I want to suggest a number of ways in which the similar experience of these two spiritual and subversive giants led to congruent positions on a number of critical issues. But these suggested congruities are not simply between Winstanley's thought and Fox's, but between True Levelling and first-generation Quakerism *en masse*. I will break these down into ten points, some more complex than can adequately be pursued here, others simple and obvious and requiring little elaboration.

One: Winstanley and Quakers shared an overwhelming conviction that the overturning times through which they were living had a cosmic dimension. God was working his purpose out through the religious, political and social tumults of the times. Three and a half centuries before Fukuyama, Winstanley and Fox believed they were witnessing the beginning of the end of history. The conviction was shared by all the sects and seekers, and notably by Cromwell. True Levellers and Quakers each subscribed to a realised eschatology which rested on a metaphorical interpretation of the Second Coming. "The rising up of Christ in sons and daughters," Winstanley writes, "is his second coming". For Fox and Friends, the second coming was Christ's indwelling power as manifested in "the people of God called by the world Quakers".

Two: For both Winstanley and Fox, the source of worldly corruption was a fallen church, led by university-educated priests who traded in the gospel as a merchant trades in corn. Anti-clericalism was rife in the forties, but nowhere more virulent and sustained than in Winstanley's writings and the Quakers' subsequent contemptuous denunciation of "hireling priests". True Levellers and Quakers opposed tithes precisely because they financed the clergy: no tithes, no clerics. For Winstanley the church was part of the "kingly power" to be overthrown, for Fox even separatist preachers like Francis Howgill and Thomas Taylor (among his earliest lieutenants) were beyond the pale till they gave up the stipends they had been paid by their Seeker congregations. Priests. whether "Common Prayer men" or Puritan "professors", were the devil's disciples. From this came Winstanley's and Fox's opposition to all church ordinances, and their advocacy of toleration, by which they meant a rooted objection to any interference by magistrates with religious belief or practice - a position learnt from the forties Baptists. Also taken straight from the Baptists was first Winstanley's, then Fox's, championing of unordained and untaught "mecanickal preachers". "The Scriptures of the Bible", Winstanley writes in *Fire in the Bush* (probably 1650), "were written by the experimentall hand of Shepherds, Husbandmen, Fishermen, and such inferiour men of the world; And the Universitie learned ones have got these mens writings; and flourishes their plaine language over with their darke interpretation, and glosses, as if it were too hard for ordinary men now to understand them; and thereby they deceive the simple, and make a prey of the poore, and cosens them of the Earth, and of the tenth of their labors '. Winstanley and Fox certainly differed when it came to church organisation: Winstanley was a congregationalist, insisting on the independence of each local church, where Fox became an ever more convinced centralist. But in their hostility to clericalism and legally enforceable prescription they were at one.

Three: Closely allied to their renunciation and denunciation of ecclesiastical authority was the conviction that, in the new dispensation, no "outward teacher" was necessary. No book (including the Bible), no sermon, no ministry had any authority except in so far as it confirmed what the reader or hearer knew and understood "experimentally". At a stroke, this undercut all academic, expert and learned authority, as well as all processes of systematic reasoning, analysis and logic, despised as producing mere "notions". Baptists and other sectaries in the mid-forties were fond of quoting Jeremiah 31: 33-4, which had prophesied a time to come when the law would be "written in men's hearts... And they shall teach no more every man his neighbour... saying Know the Lord". This has proven a great misfortune for historians, since it discouraged the sectaries from ever admitting that they had learned anything from a book or a human teacher, which greatly complicates attempts to plot influences and connections. Winstanley mentions only one man, William Everard, with whom he was associated, and Fox notoriously cites hundred whom he "convinced", but none who ever convinced him of anything. In *The Mysterie of God* in 1648 Winstanley is at pains to make it clear that what he has to say he knows "first, by my own experience", and this is contrasted with the mere book-learning of the educated clergy: "He that preaches from the book and not from the annointing is no true minister but a hireling that preaches only to get a temporary living". What he knows he knows experientially or "experimentally". Compare Fox over and over again: "And this I knew experimentally".

It is worth recalling that the language of experience and experiment was a very contemporary phenomenon. What was to become the Royal Society ("for Improving Natural Knowledge") started meeting in 1645, just three years before Winstanley first broke into print, its aim being to explore "experimental philosophy" and promote "experimental learning". This was the language of emergent science: a thing was true if it worked, and whether it worked was tested by experiment. First Winstanley and then Fox were using the newly-fashionable language of the day to revolutionise attitudes to religious authority, just as Newton and his "natural philosophers" were using it to displace superstition by science.

Four: For Winstanley as for the Quakers, the inward teacher was God or Christ, often symbolised as an inner "light". Winstanley, before Fox and

Friends, urges the importance of "walking in the light": The enlightened "come to see the spirituall Light that is in every creature, and in that power and light do walk righteously towards other creatures, as well beasts as man-kinde" (*New Law of Righteousness*, 1649).

Although neither Winstanley nor Fox acknowledge their influence, the works of the continental mystics Henry Niclaes and Jacob Boehme made repeated use of light symbolism (elaborated, of course, from John's Gospel). Significantly, the works of both Niclaes and Boehme began to appear in English translations in 1646 and, perhaps more significantly, those of Niclaes were printed by Winstanley's and Fox's printer, Giles Calvert. God is spoken of as an "inner light" by mid-forties radical Baptists, though the revolutionary implications of seeing God as within rather than without soon frightened off the Baptist hierarchy, which by 1650 was vehemently condemning the spiritual anarchy of "a God within, and a Christ within, and a word within". Winstanley was branded an atheist for insisting that there was no outward God, and Fox's imprisonment for blasphemy in 1650 followed his claim that God was in him, as in Christ. George Sabine in his Introduction to *The Works of Gerrard Winstanley* (1965) (from which all my Winstanley citations are taken) comments that the resemblance between Winstanley's and Quaker perceptions of the immanent God "is astonishingly close", and "closest of all perhaps in the case of George Fox himself, whose sense of 'Christ within', of worship as communion with God, and of such communion as an inward source of serenity and energy seems almost identical to Winstanley's conception". If there is a difference, it is that Winstanley sees God as an indwelling power in both humankind and nature - a pantheist (or panentheist) vision - whereas Fox focuses on "that of God in every man'. Winstanley's eco-centrism prefigured modern Creation Spirituality: Fox's merging of the human and the divine prefigured modern religious humanism.

It is worth noting that the " inward light" motif, which quickly became the most distinctive mark of Quakerism, was appropriated as much from emergent science and contemporary art as from Niclaes' Family of Love and Boehme's works of misty mysticism. Descartes philosophically and Newton experimentally were much preoccupied with the newly-discovered properties of light. Rembrandt, exploring the contrasts between painted oceans of light and oceans of darkness to penetrate mystery and heighten emotional response, and Vermeer, who was already experimenting with a *camera obscura* to organise his light on canvass, had both made light a fashionable subject. Again, we find Winstanley and Fox right up there with the latest trends and preoccupations.

Five: Almost as important as the "light" in Fox's theology is the "seed", which recurs again and again in the *Journal*. But here too we find Winstanley anticipating him. In *Fire in the Bush* (1649 or 1650) he writes of "the Seed or blessing" which will "rise up... to work deliverance"; and again, "they that are at liberty within, in whom the Seed is risen to rule, doe conquer all enemies by Love and patience...The Seed or Christ then is to be seen within, to save you from the curse within, to free you from bondage within; he is no Saviour that stands at a distance". For both Winstanley and Fox, the seed is a multiple metaphor: it is the Biblical promise to Abraham, but it is also a saving power within, and yet again it is the people themselves in whom Christ has risen: for Winstanley, all True Levelling communists, for Fox, "the elect seed of God called Quakers" (*Journal*, Nickalls 1975 ed., p281).

Six: Winstanley and Fox had similarly radical deconstructionist attitudes to the scriptures. Each man knew his Bible intimately, and the writings of both are saturated in biblical imagery, but both valued "experimental knowledge" far above Bible teaching. For Winstanley, scripture had value as a record of the experiences of spiritually-minded men and women in far-off times and places, and (like Fox) he wasn't above a bit of Bible-bashing himself when specifically addressing the churches. In his early works he elaborately allegorised Biblical passages, much as Niclaes and Boehme had done, though later his interest in using texts as scriptural battering-rams waned.

When Cromwell quoted scripture at him, Fox retorted that "all Christendom (so-called) had the Scriptures, but they wanted the power and the Spirit that those had who gave forth the Scriptures". Fox's university-educated friend and Friend Samuel Fisher put it more boldly: it was silly to call the Bible the Word of God, since it had no more authority than the Koran. It was "a bulk of heterogeneous writings, compiled together by men taking what they could find of the several sorts of writings that are therein, and... crowding them into a canon, or standard for the trial of spirits, doctrines, truths" (*The Rustics Alarm*, 1660). Fisher's book, comments Christopher Hill, is "a remarkable work of popular Biblical criticism, based on real scholarship. Its effect is to demote the Bible from its central position in the protestant scheme of things, to make it a book like any other book" - which is exactly what it was to Winstanley. The Bible, he said, usefully illustrated truths of which one was already convinced by experiment. Fox said much the same: "What the Lord opened to me, I afterwards found was agreeable" to scripture.

Sabine is worth quoting again, since what he says of Winstanley could equally well be inferred from Fox's teaching: "Winstanley's belief in the sufficiency of an experimental religion, consistently carried out, made a clean sweep of the mythology of the Christian tradition, and more particularly of Protestant bibliolatry. By placing the whole religious drama within the setting of the human mind, the mystics quite destroyed the external or, so to speak, the physical existence of those entities upon which all doctrinal forms of Christianity depended. Christ and the devil, Winstanley says over and over again, are not forces outside human nature; they are the impulsions and inclinations, respectively, of good and evil - the flesh and the spirit - which every man experiences as the controlling motives of his own action. The Devil is not 'a middle power between God and me, but it is the power of my proud flesh'. And 'the power of the perfect law taking hold thereupon threw me under sorrow and sealed up my misery, and this is utter darkness'. Heaven and Hell are therefore located within the soul; they are not places far off. Similarly, Christ is the generating power of goodness within every man, not the historical character who lived long ago in Palestine." Sabine quotes from Winstanley's *The Saints Paradice*, (1648): "And therefore if you expect or look for the resurrection of Jesus Christ, you must know that the spirit within the flesh is Jesus Christ, and you must see, feel, and know from himself his own resurrection within you, if you expect life and peace by him. So that you do not look for a God now, as formerly you did, to be [in] a place of glory beyond the sun, moon, and stars, nor imagine a divine being you know not where, but you see him ruling within you, and not only in you, but you see him to be the spirit and power that dwells in every man and woman; yea, in every creature, according to his orb, within the globe of the creation."

It was this insistence on dispensing with literal interpretations of the Bible, this creative impulse not only to allegorise scripture but to mine it for new myths and stories appropriate to a new dispensation, which severed both Winstanley and the Quakers from mainstream puritanism and the established Christian tradition. Neither Winstanley nor Fox invented scriptural allegorisation: it had a long history in the underground movements of the "Everlasting Gospel". But they both dragged it from under ground, brought it into the light, and used it as a double-edged sword to lay into biblical literalism and bibliolatry.

Seven: There are striking similarities in Winstanley's and Fox's theologies of resistance in relation to the use of force. This is a complex matter. Neither man, at least before the 1660s, was what we would now call a pacifist: both believed that the New Model Army was a necessary instrument of revolution. But both were unequivocal in their advocacy of non-violence, or turning the other cheek, when they and their followers were under attack, and both saw non-violence as the mark of those within whom Christ had risen.

Since the discovery by Profesor G E Aylmer in 1968 of Winstanley's early-1650 pamphlet *Englands Spirit Unfoulded*, it has been clear that Winstanley supported Cromwell's Engagement, which rested on the victories of the army and its *de facto* rule. When Winstanley attacked the army, as he frequently did, it was not for its reliance on the sword but for its failure to enforce a revolutionary settlement. Winstanley saw the army as the vanguard of the poor, and it was his faith and hope that Christ would rise in and through the revolutionary regime, not in spite of it. The Council of State was the agency which would deliver freedom, not the obstacle to freedom. Fox's position, at least before 1660, was similar. Although he had declined the offer of a commission in 1651, by 1652 he was deliberately targeting the military for Quaker recruits (see my article "The Quaker Military Alliance" in *Friends Quarterly*, October 1997, reprinted in this booklet, page 89, which examines the close connections between early Friends and the New Model Army). As late as 1658 he is lambasting Cromwell for not carrying his republican crusade into Holland, Germany, Spain, Turkey and the Vatican itself, urging "Let thy soldiers go forth... that thou may rock nations as a cradle". For Margaret Fell too, the army was "the Battle-axe in the hand of the Lord".

But while True Levellers in the forties and Quakers in the fifties saw military power as the indispensable guarantee of republican freedom, which in turn was the foundation of the "New Heaven and New Earth" which they believed they had been called to build, both movements renounced the use of violence to further their own ends, even in self-defence. Before starting his communist experiment, Winstanley had written in *The New Law of Righteousness*: "The Lord himself will do this great work, without either sword or weapon; weapons and swords shall destroy, and cut the powers of the earth asunder, but they shall never build up". When the Cobham community was repeatedly attacked, its members beaten, its houses burnt, its crops uprooted, Winstanley insisted that retaliation of any kind was not an option for those in whom Christ had risen. "For my part, and for the rest [of the Diggers]", he writes in *A New-yeers Gift* (1650), "we abhor fighting for Freedom, it is acting of the Curse and lifting him up higher; and do thou uphold it by the Sword, we will not, we will conquer by Love and Patience, or else we count it no Freedom: Freedom gotten by the Sword is an established bondage to some part or other of the Creation; and this we have declared publickly enough... Victory that is gotten by the Sword, is a Victory that slaves gets one over another;... but Victory obtained by Love, is a Victory for a King... This great Leveller, Christ our King of righteousness in us, shall cause men to beat their swords into plowshares, and spears into pruning hooks..." In *The True Levellers Standard Advanced* (1649), written after the first mob attacks on his commune, Winstanley declares that they are willing to shed their own blood, but not that of their enemies: "We shall not do this by force of Armes, we abhorre it". And when his community was finally routed and dispersed, he writes: "We have declared our Testimony, and now let freedom and bondage strive who shall rule in Mankind: the weapons of the Sonnes of bondage being carnall, as fire, club and sword; the weapons of the Sonnes of freedom being spirituall, as love, patience and righteousness".

In his last book, *The Law of Freedom*, where he attempts a constitution for a state which has adopted common ownership of the land, Winstanley does allow for armed defence, and for capital punishment for serious offences. Early Friends also tacitly accepted that a state dedicated to the building of heaven on earth had the right and duty to defend itself against God's enemies, and it was many years before they began to challenge capital punishment. In only one important and somewhat bizarre respect did Winstanley's teaching differ sharply from Fox's: *The Law of Freedom* advocated capital punishment for preachers who accepted payment for their trade. Such "shall be put to death for a witch and a cheater".

This apart, the active non-resistance of the True Levellers closely prefigures that of Friends. "Like George Fox", writes Sabine, "...Winstanley distrusted the efficacy of force to accomplish any permanent moral results, and this was altogether in accord with the belief that morality begins with a change of heart. Hence the root of moral regeneration is a kind of passivity, submissiveness of the better impulse that will rise if it be given the chance, a silence and a waiting until the wiser thought and action ripens". Here is the essence of what became Quaker pacifism, and it is at the heart of everything Winstanley wrote and enacted.

Eight: Not only does Winstanley's theology of nonviolence prefigure Fox's, but so too does some of the graphic imagery with which it is advanced. Quakers made much of the imagery of "the Lamb's war" to describe their own militant engagement with the "beast", the "dragon". But Winstanley was there before them. In his *Letter to the Lord Fairfax* (1649) he writes: "In this work of Community in the earth, and in the fruits of the earth, is seen plainly a pitched battaile between the Lamb and the Dragon, between the Spirit of love, humility and righteousnesse, which is the Lamb appearing in flesh; and the power of envy, pride, and unrighteousnesse, which is the Dragon appearing in flesh". And again, in *The Bloudie and Unchristian Acting* (1649), in one of his most powerful passages: "But now O England know this, that thy striving now is not only Dragon against Dragon, Beast against Beast, Covetousnesse and Pride against Covetousnesse and Pride, but thou now begin'st to fight against the Lamb, the Dove, the meek Spirit, the power of love... The battell between the Dragon and the Lamb is begun in the midst of thee, and a few years now will let all the world see who is strongest, love or hatred, freedom or bondage". Thereafter the language of the Lamb's war is never absent from Winstanley's writings, and it is soon to find a central place in Quaker polemics.

Nine: Winstanley and Fox shared a radical social vision which was all the more threatening to the powerful in its explicit appeal to the powerless. Both men attacked the social hierarchies of church and state, both rammed home the awkward message that God's promises were to the poor and the meek. Both preached a kingdom of God on earth: salvation or freedom was for now and for this life, not for later, in some other world. Winstanley went much further than Fox in demanding full economic equality and common ownership of the land, but Fox, ten years after the True Levellers' commune, came close to matching him when he called in 1659 for the confiscation of all former monastic lands, glebes, and the great gentry estates. Fox's diatribes against the great ones who "cumbred the ground", who were "harlotted from the truth, and such gets the earth under their hands, commons, wastes and forrest, and fells and mores and mountains, and lets it lie waste, and calls themselves Lords of it, and keeps it from the people, when so many are ready to starve and beg" - all this reads like pure Winstanley. Indeed, in arguing that church buildings and Whitehall itself should be turned over to the poor, that the people should respond to tithe demands with civil disobedience, that lords of the manor should have their fines confiscated and that the gentry should be disarmed, Fox arguably went even further than Winstanley - though his revolutionary demands (with the notable exception of civil disobedience against tithes) were quietly forgotten after the Restoration, and dropped as an embarrassment from Fox's incomplete *Complete Works*.

Ten: Finally, Winstanley and Fox both had a genius for propaganda. It was Winstanley who pioneered the publication of "sufferings" to attract sympathy for his communes, and the Quakers famously made good use of the tactic. Moreover, when Gervase Benson and Anthony Pearson first published Friends' sufferings, their printer was Winstanley's: Giles Calvert.

So I now approach the critical question: are these congruities simply coincidental, the result of contemporaries drawing from the same well of dissent, or did Winstanley's writings have a direct if wholly unacknowledged influence on Fox and early Quakerism? As noted earlier, as early as 1678, two years after Winstanley's death, Thomas Comber claimed in his anti-Quaker pamphlet *Christianity no Enthusiasm* that Quakerism was but a rehash of Winstanley's teachings, which in his view made repression of Friends "not only a service to God, but a preservation of every man and his property" - perhaps the first recorded instance of an anti-communist smear campaign! As we have seen, the nineteenth-century Marxists who rediscovered Winstanley and claimed him as one of their own all suggested Quakers derived much of their distinctive theology from the True Leveller. But Quaker historians were doubtful, cautiously content, perhaps, to leave Winstanley with the Marxists. Even Richard T Vann, in his important essay charting Winstanley's journey "from radicalism to Quakerism" (*Journal of Friends Historical Society*, No. 49, 1959-61) placed more emphasis on Winstanley's movement *towards* Quakerism than on his possible role in shaping it.

But there is something oddly unsatisfactory about this notion that radical ideas somehow floated in the ether of mid seventeenth-century England, to be caught and absorbed independently by Winstanley in London and Fox in the north. Ideas are not like pollen grains, wafting about in the spring air. Ideas are born by being spoken or written, and they are spread by being heard or read. In seventeenth-century England the mass media of communication were the pulpit (professional and lay) and the printing press (official and unofficial). We are therefore entitled to a little healthy scepticism about claims to learn only from an "inward teacher": or, if we don't wish to be sceptics, we are entitled to conclude that the inward teacher made efficient use of outward agents - the preachers and pamphleteers who spread the word and made it their business to turn the world upside down.

Winstanley and Fox both tell us how, as seekers, they sampled the sects, where they will have heard preachers galore. They tell us virtually nothing, however, of what they read. But are we to suppose that the unprecedented flood of pamphlets, of political and religious debate in the newly-emergent free press, simply passed them by? That they read only their Bibles? That Winstanley clung so faithfully to his inward teacher that he never strayed into the books in Sarah Gates' theological library, and that Fox's fidelity to his "openings" preserved him from reading anything written by his fellow-seekers? I don't believe it.

Consider: When the young, seeking George Fox was having his first "pure openings of the Light without the help of any man" (*Journal* p33) in 1648, Winstanley's first three pamphlets were streaming off Calvert's press. When Fox teamed up with Elizabeth Hooton in 1649, the news-sheets were full of Winstanley's dig, which was the talk of the country. By the time Fox was touring Yorkshire in 1651 and putting together the first building-blocks of what was to become the Quaker movement, Winstanley was working on his twentieth publication. The demand for these works was such that Calvert had to reprint several of them: *The Mysterie of God* and *the Breaking of the Day of God*, both first published in 1648, were reissued the following year, and again in 1650 when they were included in a Winstanley collection, *Several Pieces Gathered into one Volume*. Two editions of *The Saints Paradice* appeared in 1648 and another in 1649. *Truth Lifting up its Head* of 1649 was reprinted in 1650. *The New Law of Righteousness* of 1649 was reprinted the same year. It is clear that Winstanley's works had an eager readership, and those readers must surely have been the very radicals, seekers and separatists in whose excited, enthusiastic meetings early Quakerism was at that very moment taking root. It is hard to believe that Fox himself was not among those readers.

To what extent the congruities and similarities of Winstanley's and Fox's writings were the result of serendipity or direct influence remains hard to pin down. It is clear that both men derived much of their distinctive teaching from common sources such as the teachings of Niclaes and Boehme (not to mention John's Gospel and the Book of Revelation), the theological radicalism of "shattered Baptists" and seekers and the social radicalism of the Lilburne Levellers (a group quite distinct from the True Levellers). But the startling similarity of language and imagery strongly suggests that Fox knew Winstanley's works. The fact that these works were being published at the precise time when Fox was beginning to give shape to his own ideas, and issued from the same press which was soon to publicise Quakerism, make a degree of direct influence highly probable. Thus both the internal and the external evidence combine to suggest that the inward teacher benefited from a helping hand. Fox knew what he knew experimentally: but his experience surely included reading and absorbing the inspirational words of his immediate predecessor, who lived and died in the hope that Christ, the spirit of love and community, might yet rise in sons and daughters.

It is clear to me that Winstanley the True Leveller was a formative influence on early Quakerism, a maker of the tradition we have inherited. We should pay him more attention than we have done hitherto. And we could begin by identifying his burial place and agitating for the erection of a plaque to honour this extraordinary pioneer of social justice, non-violence, and religious humanism.

The Quaker Military Alliance

First published in "Friends Quarterly", October 1997, based on a paper for the Quaker Studies Research Association

An alliance between peace-loving Friends and the armed forces? Some mistake, surely?

I want to draw attention to an aspect of Quaker history which until recently has been largely overlooked by both non-Quaker and Quaker historians: by non-Quakers (with some notable exceptions like Christopher Hill and Barry Reay) because they have tended to underestimate the part played by Friends in the English revolution, and by Quaker historians, either because they have a distaste for the militant republican Quakerism of the 1650s or because they judge a Quakerism concerned with building a New Earth as less mature and less valuable than a Quakerism not of this world.

Imagine that we are looking at the history of Quakerism, not from our present-day perspective but from that of March 1660. England has been a republic for just over ten years. Quakers have been an organised body within the republic for eight of those ten years. We do not yet know that before the leaves return to the trees the revolution will collapse, the republic will be finished, and the old order of king, lords and bishops which we thought had been done away with for ever will be back with a vengeance. Still less can we have any notion that within a year those militant Quakers who tried so hard to turn the world upside down, and who backed Cromwell's military dictatorship because they were convinced that his sword was wielded on God's behalf, will do a U-turn and "utterly deny... all outward wars and strife and fightings with outward weapons for any end or under any pretence whatsoever".

In this article I am concerned solely with the 1650s. We need to remind ourselves that in this, their pioneering decade, Quakers, including George Fox, were not yet pacifists; that they supported Cromwell's armed rule for much of the decade; that they served the republic as soldiers and naval officers; that they were widely perceived by their contemporaries, friends and enemies alike, as representing the radical or left wing of the armed revolution, in alliance with the army; and that this perception, far from being a calumny invented by the Quakers' enemies, was a fair reading of their position.

It is not my intention to argue that there is some kind of pure, true Quakerism which embraces armed conflict and to which we should seek to return! There are many aspects of early Quakerism - its intolerance of both external and internal dissent, its extravagances such as walking naked through the streets crying "Woe to Yorkshire" (or wherever), its hostility to the arts, its repressed and repressive attitude to sexual expression - which no Friend today would wish to resurrect. My aim here is a view of early Quaker history which is consistent with the documentary evidence, whether or not we find it agreeable to our modern sensibilities.

While George Fox was a growing lad in Leicestershire in the 1630s a long-simmering conflict was coming to a head. Who had authority to rule, in the state and in the church? The king and his court and bishops, or the people, represented in parliament? In 1642 the quarrel became a civil war, with the king and the established church in one corner and parliament and the puritan reformers in the other. The first round saw parliament and puritans in the ascendant, depriving the king of effective power and abolishing the episcopal Church of England. But then the parliamentary-puritan side started quarrelling among themselves. What we might now call "moderate" or "right-wing" puritans wanted to replace the established Anglican church with an established presbyterian system under a reformed monarchy. The "left" wanted a decentralised church, an "Independent" system in which dissent (within limits) was tolerated, and the crown was either subordinated to parliament or done away with altogether.

The conflict within the parliamentary-puritan party came to a head when Cromwell and his Independent colleagues won control of military operations and created the New Model Army in 1645. What was new about the New Model was that its leadership - its officers, cavalry and chaplains - were deliberately and systematically recruited from the ranks of the "godly": Independents, Baptists and separatists with revolutionary views on politics and religion. They were soldiers from conviction rather than conscription and compulsion, men who in Cromwell's words "had the fear of God before them and made some conscience of what they did". They prayed, studied the Bible and worshipped together without sanction of priest or church. They agitated for democracy, for the abolition of tithes to drive priests out of business, and for the overthrow of the aristocracy. There was never an army like it before, and as Noel Brailsford has commented in *The Levellers and the English Revolution*, "nor was there anything like it thereafter till the Workers' and Soldiers' Councils met in 1917 in Russia" - though, so far as we know, the Russian workers and soldiers didn't hold prayer meetings.

By 1648 the presbyterian gentry were so alarmed by the army's religious and revolutionary zeal that the bulk of them defected to the king as protector of traditional property and power structures. So the last phases of the civil war saw Independents pitted against the combined forces of the old royalist party, the presbyterian defectors and the Scots. The king now had numbers on his side, but Cromwell had the New Model Army. The king was captured, tried and beheaded, and by 1651, after the battle of Worcester, the kingdom of England was dead too, reborn as a New Model Republic which entrusted its peace to the godly soldiers of the New Model Army.

Many early Quakers, including members of the movement's core founding group, took up the sword in the service of the revolution. James Nayler was nine years a soldier, serving as Major-General Lambert's quartermaster. Preaching to his troops after the battle of Dunbar in September 1650, Nayler so impressed one of Cromwell's officers that he was "afraid to stay, for I was made a Quaker!". Note that Nayler was "making Quakers" before he ever met or heard of George Fox. The very first Quakers, it seems, were made in the New Model Army. William Dewsbury joined the army "in obedience to God", and after sampling the Independents and the Baptists found his mind turned within to the light of his conscience. This was as early as 1645. He called himself a Quaker by 1651. Richard Farnsworth claimed of himself that there was "no more ardent Roundhead" in his district, when the term Roundhead was a term of abuse for parliamentary soldiers. William C. Braithwaite speculates that it was this group - Nayler, Dewsbury and Farnsworth - who invited George Fox to the North in 1651.

According to Barry Reay's important study *The Quakers and the English Revolution* - largely neglected by Friends with a distaste for historical revisionism - scores more prominent early Friends were soldiers. Richard Hubberthorne, Edward Billing, John Crook, Gervase Benson, Edward Cook, Amos Stoddart, William Morris, Thomas Curtis, George Bishop (whose 1659 tract *To the General Council of the Army* called on the generals to reinstate Friends purged from the forces), Edward Pyott, Francis Gawler, Joseph Fuce: all these were officers. The other George Fox known as "the younger", Benjamin Nicholson, William Edmundson, John Whitehead,

John and Thomas Stubbs and William Ames served in the ranks. American historian Richard Vann refers to 95 Quakers who served in the army, but there were hundreds more.

Fox, of course, never joined up, and he tells us in his Journal that he specifically refused a pressing invitation to take a commission offered in 1651 - something I shall return to later. But let us first look carefully at the company he was keeping, and at the men he chose to target as he began to weld into one movement the disparate groups variously called Seekers, "shattered Baptists", Ranters and Quakers in the autumn of 1651 and spring of 1652.

Released from Derby jail in October 1651 after serving nearly a year for contravening the Blasphemy Act, Fox made his way to Yorkshire, either by their invitation or providentially meeting up with the Nayler-Dewsbury-Farnsworth group of ex-soldiers, newly demobilised after the "crowning mercy" of the battle of Worcester. This historic meeting, which brought together the six young men (the other two were Thomas Aldam and Thomas Goodaire) who organised the first great Quaker missionary journeys in the north, was held at the home of one *Lieutenant* Roper. As Fox moves on, he targets and makes converts of army *Captain* Richard Pursloe of Cranswick, near Selby, and his friend Justice Durant Hotham, who was to act as his protector. After criss-crossing Yorkshire and "convincing many'" Fox has a "great meeting" at the house of *Colonel* Robert Overton. After climbing Pendle Hill, Fox makes his way northwards to Dent, where among the few who are convinced is *Captain* Alexander Hebblethwaite. Next stop Garsdale, where he searches out *Major* Miles Bousfield. On to Sedbergh and Brigflatts, where he makes for the home of army veteran Richard Robinson, who takes him to a meeting at Borret, the home of *Captain* Gervase Benson, the regional military commissioner. Among the Westmorland Seekers, Fox convinces *Captain* Henry Ward of Grayrigg, and other Seekers Fox meets for the first time are outspoken republican zealots: Richard Hubberthorne, Edward Burrough, Thomas Taylor. On his way to Swarthmoor Hall he searches out *Captain* Adam Sandys of Bouth, chief constable of Ulverston (but finds him "a very chaffy light man... for his god was his belly"). At Swarthmoor he has clearly targeted Justice Thomas Fell, Cromwell's leading man in the far north-west, Vice-Chancellor of the Duchy of Lancaster and friend and circuit-colleague of Judge John Bradshaw who, as President of the court which condemned Charles Stuart to death, was the midwife of the republic itself. Fell had turned over part of his Swarthmoor home as a billet for New Model Army troops.

Let's convert this into statistics. There are 46 men Fox names (or whose names have been added as footnotes by his editors) in his Pendle-to-Swarthmoor narrative - the mythic origin of the Quaker movement. Thirteen of these are "priests" or JPs who may or may not have had direct military connections. Of the remaining 33, no fewer than 20 - well over half - carry a military rank, or are known from other sources to have been in the army or connected with it. Of course, some of the remaining 13 may also have served in the army although there is no specific mention of it. However we compute it, army men are strongly and disproportionately represented in this account. What, then, might we infer from this?

It seems clear that Fox was recommended from one group and one individual to another. From the Pendle inn where he stayed after his climb, he tells us he had the innkeeper and his wife send out papers advertising his presence in the area. We may reasonably guess that the unnamed kinsman of John Blaykling whom he met near Wensleydale told him of the Dent Independents (who were organising a tithe strike at the time) and their leader Captain Hebblethwaite, who told him of Major Bousfield in Garsdale, who told him of Richard Robinson and Captain Benson in Sedbergh, who certainly introduced him to the Westmorland Seekers, who perhaps told him of Captain Sandys of Bouth and Justice Fell of Swarthmoor. Fox wasn't blundering around aimlessly, guided by some kind of blind divine intuition. He networked his way across the northwest, following the recommendations of sympathisers and targeting influential men with the radical sympathies which might make them receptive to the Quaker message. Most of these men were clearly the military leaders of their local communities, guardians of the new English republic.

It may be objected that some of the men named were *former* soldiers, no longer in active service, and even those who were still known by their army rank may no longer have been serving officers by 1652. Why should we assume that Fox's targeting of these men implies some kind of Quaker-military alliance? May it not be the case that Fox opened their eyes to the futility and wickedness of a military life, turning them from Cromwellian soldiers into Quaker pacifists?

There are two answers to that. One is that Quakers continued to serve in the army, and also the navy, all through the 1650s. But there is another point to be made with respect to Fox himself. It is striking that, of the many recorded occasions when he meets these captains and majors, not once does he rebuke them for their calling, for their use of "carnal weapons". He objects to Captain Sandys' sense of humour and his appetite for the good life, both of which he thinks inappropriate for a puritan, but he does not criticise the captain's military profession. Is it not surprising that the man who is to become best known to the world as the pacifist leader of a pacifist sect breathes not one recorded word of criticism of the soldiers' trade?

But what about the occasion in 1651 when Fox specifically refused a commission? In April of that year, with the decisive battle of Worcester looming, he was visited in Derby jail by the army commissioners urging him to accept appointment as a captain. "They proffered me that preferment because of my virtue", he says in the Journal, "with many other compliments, and asked me if I would not take up arms for the Commonwealth against the King". And he famously replied: "I told them I lived in the virtue of that life and power that took away the occasion of all wars, and I knew from whence all wars did rise, from the lust according to James's doctrine [a reference to James iv, 1]. I told them I was come into the covenant of peace which was before wars and strikes were."

The first point I want to make here is one which is often missed. While Fox emphasised that he refused the commission, I want to make the point that *it was offered*. What is striking, surely, is that the New Model recruitment panel clearly recognised a fellow-zealot for the republican cause. They praised his "virtue" - which John Nickalls, the modern editor of the Journal, translates as "valour". They heaped compliments on him. They were clearly familiar with what he had done, said, believed, preached. He might be an extremist, but he was their kind of extremist: "one of us". He opposed tithes: so did they. He championed the poor: so did they. He proposed to eliminate every lord and aristocrat from England: so did they. He did all he could to undermine the power of the national church: so did they. His radical politics and his radical religion were interfused, inseparable - as were the politics and religion of the Levellers, the army Agitators and the junior officers of the New Model. He was for the English revolution, God's own cause, and that was enough.

But let us focus on his answer: "I lived in the virtue of that life and power that took away the occasion of all wars". This sounds like pacifism. It seems to anticipate by a full decade the peace testimony of Restoration Quakerism.

It has generally been interpreted as indicating that, even if other Quakers were slower to abandon the sword, Fox himself was clear on the necessity of renouncing force right from the start, and had to wait ten years for the rest of the movement to catch up with him. But this interpretation will not do. It squares with the Journal, dictated many years later, but not with what Fox was writing and publishing in the 1650s.

Christopher Hill ventured the suggestion, when he addressed the George Fox Tercentenary Conference in Lancaster in 1991, that Fox unconsciously projected his 1670s pacifism back into the 1650s. Another explanation, I suggest, is that Fox refused the commission not because he objected in principle to the use of military force in a godly cause but because he believed God had chosen him personally for something different. He supported the army, but did not himself feel called to be a soldier.

Those who insist that we must take the absolute pacifism of Fox's 1651 statement (as recalled and written down in 1675) at face value, must address several problems. The first is the one I have already dealt with at some length: that Fox appears to have targeted the military as the very people most likely to be sympathetic to his message, without ever suggesting they should renounce their military calling. But if that is deemed inconclusive, consider this message to Cromwell, signed "George Fox" and dated January 1658, where the Protector is lambasted for not carrying his military conquests into Europe and on to Rome itself – even to the Turkish empire:

"Oliver, hadst thou been faithful and thundered down the deceit, the Hollander had been thy subject and tributary, Germany had given up to have done thy will, and the Spaniard had quivered like a dry leaf wanting the virtue of God, the King of France should have bowed his neck under thee, the Pope should have withered as in winter, the Turk in all his fatness should have smoked, thou shouldst not have stood trifling about small things, but minded the work of the Lord as He began with thee at first ... Let thy soldiers go forth... that thou may rock nations as a cradle."

It is very hard to read this as a pacifist tract! Interestingly, it was not included when Fox's collected works were published after his death. The original parchment is at Friends House, London (Bound Parchment Portfolio 9, p79). Edward Burrough quoted it approvingly in his pamphlet *Good Counsel and Advice Rejected* in 1659.

In another pamphlet, *To the Council of Officers of the Armie,* probably published in 1659, Fox urges the troops to "see that you know a soldier's place... and that ye be soldiers qualified". One Quaker soldier, he asserted, was worth seven non-Quakers. If the army grandees could not be trusted to see the work through, "the inferior officers and soldiers" should take on the task themselves. Addressing them over the heads of their generals, he urged them "never set up your standard till you come to Rome". Indulging a surprising military fantasy, he railed against the army for failing to invade Spain and root out the Inquisition, and for holding back from a conquest of the Turkish empire which would have released the innocent from "thralldom, bondage and captivity". Clearly for the young George Fox the sword had its place in fulfilling God's purpose on earth, even if he personally felt called - as he clearly did - to a different way of life.

Christopher Hill in his Lancaster address reminded us of other contemporary statements of Quaker support for republican military rule. Friends "stood by [Cromwell] in time of greatest dangers in all the late wars", wrote Francis Howgill, adding that "many precious men ventured their lives and lost their blood" to win liberty "as men and Christians". James Nayler agreed. When there were moves to silence Quakers after Cromwell's death in 1658, Nayler protested that Friends "generally did venture their lives and estates with those that are in the present government, purchasing their freedom as men with great loss". No doubt he spoke with feeling: he had spent nine years fighting under Lambert. George Bishop, who as an army captain and Agitator had dared accuse the high command of not being wholeheartedly republican, defended the king's execution "for the preservation of the public interest". He told Cromwell in 1656 that the republican cause was "the highest on which men were ever engaged in the field". Edward Burrough believed it was God, working through the army, who "overthrew that oppressing power of king, lords... and bishops, and brought some tyrants and oppressors to just execution". In 1659 he declared himself "given to believe that there is some great work to do by them, in their nations, with their outward sword, and that time is not long till a good thing may be accomplished by our English army". Even Quakerism's nursing-mother-superior Margaret Fell described the army as "the Battle-axe in the hand of the Lord", telling the military leadership in her 1659 pamphlet *To the General Councel and Officers of the Army* that "though we [Quakers] be but little and small in your eyes... yet it will be good for you, if ye have our prayers".

Few Quaker soldiers resigned from the army when they were convinced. William Dewsbury did so, apparently on genuine pacifist grounds, but that was before he became a Quaker; and Edward Billing resigned his position as a cornet in General Monck's army to become a Quaker brewer, though he made it clear he still "owned the sword in its place". But they were the exceptions. Barry Reay finds evidence of Quaker recruitment in the army garrisons in York, Bristol, Holy Island and Berwick-upon-Tweed, Lancaster, Carlisle, Chester, Kent, Northamptonshire, Norfolk, Shrewsbury and London.

Friends were particularly successful in making Quakers of the soldiers in Cromwell's army of conquest in Ireland in 1655 and 1656, with one officer, Colonel Nicholas Kempson, promising to build a meetinghouse in Cavan, another provincial governor, Richard Hodden of Kinsale, appointing a Quaker minister to preach to his troops, and another, Governor Robert Phayre of Cork, reporting that "more is done by the Quakers than all the priests in the country have done in a hundred years". Many Quakers were also recruited in the army in Scotland. True, both Henry Cromwell in Ireland and General Monck in Scotland moved against Quakers and tried to purge them from their armies, but not because they were pacifist; on the contrary, because they were considered dangerously militant and potentially mutinous. Also, their insistence on treating everyone equally, and therefore refusing the usual compliments due to officers, was considered prejudicial to good order and discipline. In 1657 a non-Quaker colonel complained that his captain was "much confirmed in his principle of quaking, making all the soldiers his equal (according to the Levellers' strain)". This captain even forbade his men to salute him, which the colonel thought "the root of disobedience" and "anarchy", since "where all are equals I expect little obedience". Quakers bitterly opposed the purges and struggled hard to stay within the army's ranks. When Monck purged forty Quakers from his forces in 1657, none had been in the army less than seven years and the majority had service records of fourteen years, which means they had joined up at the beginning of the civil war and had remained soldiers during Cromwell's military dictatorship.

In the crisis year of 1659, when it became clear that the half-way revolution was no longer an option, when England must either settle the republic on a permanent basis or fall back into royalist reaction, Quakers were in the forefront of those who adopted a militant revolutionary position. When the army restored the Rump of the Long Parliament to power, George Fox exulted: "the Lord Jesus is come to reign... Now shall the Lamb and the saints have victory". Edward Burrough, in an address to the army omitted from his collected works as later published by Friends, declared "We look for a New Earth as well as for a New Heaven", adding that Quakers expected the army and Parliament together to secure the "just freedom of the people". Quaker naval captain Anthony Mellidge drew on Leveller language to remind his masters that this freedom had been won by bloody warfare: "We are not only free-born of England, but we have also purchased our freedom in the nation, and the continuation thereof, with many years hard service, the loss of the lives of many hundreds, the spoiling of much goods, and the shedding of much blood in the late war, by which at last the Lord overturned them".

It was at this critical stage that Fox produced the most revolutionary political programme ever published by a Quaker leader, calling not only for the standard Leveller package of toleration, abolition of tithes and law reform, but also for a huge programme of public ownership by way of the wholesale expropriation of church and crown lands, royalists' property, and estates once held by the monasteries and now enjoyed by the gentry. This, coupled with the confiscation of manorial profits, would finance a radical new system of poor relief and the maintenance of a standing army, which Fox saw as the guarantee of the revolutionary Commonwealth. But the restored Rump failed to respond or produce the liberties demanded. (And Friends decided not to include this pamphlet, *To the Parliament of the Commonwealth of England: Fifty-nine Particulars*, in his collected works).

There were rumours of royalist uprisings, and Parliament moved to set up new local militias in which Quakers were active. General Lambert recruited northern Friends to help crush "Booth's Rebellion" in Cheshire, though Fox, in a sudden volte face, now chastised the "foolish, rash spirits" among Friends who still clung to hopes of military salvation. But his was something of a lone voice among the radicals. The only hope now for the party which sought a New Heaven, declared Henry Stubbe, was that it was "possessed with the militia of the nation, and under good commanders". When the Rump fell and control reverted to the army and its Committee of Safety, the rush into the militias increased. Quaker Anthony Pearson set about recruiting an armed force from among Kendal and Lancaster Friends. Five Friends were named commissioners for the Westminster militia, two for Berkshire, and one each for Cheshire, Cornwall, Devon, Gloucestershire, Glamorgan, Worcestershire and Wiltshire. Five Quaker leaders in Bristol served as commissioners there, and six in North-West Wales. Barry Reay argues that it was the spectre of the Quakers seizing power, reintroducing the demands of the Levellers (as augmented by Fox's newly published programme), and reopening the wounds of the civil wars that panicked the gentry into the camp which would restore monarchy the following year.

Quaker leaders like Francis Howgill, Edward Burrough and George Bishop actively supported direct resistance to the counter-revolution. But later in that same fateful year of 1659, when the political struggle was nearing its climax, Fox seems to have withdrawn from the struggle in growing disillusionment. When Bristol Friends asked his opinion on whether Friends could serve as soldiers he answered half-heartedly that "there is something in the thing... and you cannot well leave them seeing you have gone among them". A little later when Welsh Friends asked the same question, his answer is not recorded in any contemporary document, but he tells us later he "forbade" it.

In the very last days of the republic, Fox records in the Journal that while riding out on his horse in Nottinghamshire he was met by a troop of soldiers on their way to join General Lambert in a last-ditch stand against Monck's troops who were marching south to put Charles II on the throne. Lambert's republicans wanted to buy Fox's horse, but he refused to sell, telling them that "God would confound and scatter them" - as indeed he did in the next few days. For Fox, the Quaker-military alliance was over - even if Lambert's army still had many Quaker soldiers in it.

Of course Friends had never been entirely at one with the various republican governments of the 1650s. The wider struggle for a godly Commonwealth was for them only part of their own "Lamb's War". They formed the left wing of a revolution to which the leaders of those governments paid lip-service, while constantly trying to hold it in check. Nearly two thousand Quakers were imprisoned during Cromwell's regime, mostly by local authorities where revolutionary loyalties were thin. But the middle ranks of the army no less than the Quakers remained a radical stronghold, at least until 1657, and whenever the revolution looked set to go into reverse Quakers and the military made common cause. In 1659 Friends seem to have tried briefly to take over the army, as the Levellers had tried in 1648 and the Fifth Monarchists in 1653, and with the same lack of success.

The alliance was shattered when the revolution collapsed and the monarchy was restored. From being the critical left wing of the ruling party and allies of the ruling army, Quakers were singled out as the most intransigent enemies of the crown. Their response was to declare themselves harmless, meeting accusations of plotting with the peace declarations of 1660 and 1661. Quaker politics increasingly took a new form, that of passive resistance and mass civil disobedience, undertaken against the new king in the name of a King of kings who was not of this world. There was no place for the sword in this kind of politics, and the old alliance with the army was not only abandoned but rapidly written out of Quaker history.

It is no part of my argument that the peace testimony is somehow less valid because it resulted from a Quaker U-turn. Indeed, the fact that it grew out of long and bitter experience of the failure of armed struggle to create a New Earth surely gives it more rather than less potency. In any case, while rejection of "carnal weapons" clearly represented a political U-turn, it may also be seen as a natural development of Friends' consistent refusal to return violence for violence on the personal level, a testimony to which they were conscientiously attached even when allied with the army. Counter-revolution in 1660 proved that hopes of an earthly reign of the saints, a New Model theocracy, were false, and Friends found themselves forging a new politics of survival in an unregenerate world where paradise was postponed indefinitely.

But the fact of the Quaker-military alliance during the English Republic should alert us to the inadequacy of the received version of our history, which has been so filtered, censored, distorted, re-invented, that it now misleads more than it leads. If we are going to make a serious effort to understand Quaker religious experience in the seventeenth century, which we have to do if we are seriously interested in articulating Quaker religious experience in our own time, we must reopen the archives and study them without preconceptions and with as much objectivity as we can muster. It will not do to rely on our Quaker historians alone: even the very best, fairest and most scholarly, like William C. Braithwaite, but particularly the many who have simply recycled the old, old story. Intuition alone, that good old standby and very present help to the intellectually lazy, will avail us nothing here. Creative flair and imagination will be essential, but hard work by disciplined minds even more so. Of course every history is an interpretation, and historical truth is always relative. But we need a new narrative, and to make it we need to draw on non-Quaker and anti-Quaker as well as Quaker sources, and certainly on non-Quaker as well as Quaker historians.

I also believe we can learn something positive from the republican Quaker church-militant. Early Friends were surely right to link the making of a New Earth with a New Heaven, to recognise that if mercy, pity, peace and love are to flourish, the world - this world - must be mended and society radically refashioned. In a pre-democratic state where it seemed that the power to refashion society could only be won by force of arms, early Friends – with few exceptions – could not and did not dissociate themselves from the sword. After 1660, when Friends abandoned the sword because it had failed them, they necessarily abandoned the pursuit of political power to change the world. But in twentieth-century England the sword is no longer the sole arbiter of power. There has been a democratic revolution, incomplete and imperfect, but one which allows the pursuit of power by peaceful means. We no longer have to choose between political-action-with-violence and non-violence-with-political-withdrawal.

That means that, if we choose, we can look again at the New Earth which 1650s Friends strove to build in alliance with the New Model Army, and ask if we cannot pick up where they left off, building this time in alliance with the democratic process. Dare we resume the campaign for a society of equals, in which the power of non-elected peers and monarch are abolished and the mighty put down from their seats, a society which is not frightened to expropriate the rich to relieve the poor, a society which at last disestablishes the Church of England and deprives it of its indefensible privileges?

Now there's a Quaker programme for the twenty-first century!

Part Three

Under Review

A 'Hallowed Secularism' and the Remaking of God

This review of the novel 'City of God' by E.L.Doctorow (Little, Brown), £15.99, was published in SOF magazine, March 2001

It's high time we had a fully SoF-soaked novel, one which unmistakably reflects and interprets our postmodern angst about God and what the hell can be done about him: one which does for the SoF view of religion what *News from Nowhere* and *The Ragged-Trousered Philanthropist* did for utopian socialism, *Uncle Tom's Cabin* did for the abolition of slavery and *Anna Veronica* did for the emancipation of women. We've come within hailing distance with David Lodge's *How Far Can You Go?* and *Paradise News*, which boasted a Cupittian theologian as hero, and Jeanette Winterson's fiction inhabits an anti-realist world which rings the bells SoFers are fond of sounding. But we haven't had the Big One yet...

Till now. Till Doctorow: the New York author of *Ragtime*, and winner of more literary awards than you and I have ever heard of. *City of God* is a stunning novel of ideas, and the ideas are those which absorb, trouble, inspire, excite, scare and obsess just the kinds of people who find themselves swimming (or drowning) off Dover beach with the sound of a receding sea of faith filling their ears. What can we make of things like religion, God, and church in a post-holocaust, post-Nietzsche, post-Einstein, post-Freud and post-modern world? That's what *City of God* is about.

First, then, the story - because the ideas and themes and diversions, of which there are many, are placed within a narrative framework: this is a novel, not a treatise. Father Tom Pemberton, priest at St Timothy's Episcopal Church in Lower Manhattan, discovers one morning that the large brass cross behind his altar has gone missing. Then he gets a call from a husband-and-wife team of rabbis who run the Synagogue for Evolutionary Judaism on the Upper West Side. The cross, it seems, has been found on the synagogue roof. So who dunnit? Zionists? Right-wing anti-Semites? Nutters? Is it a prank, or an omen?

Now it happens that Father Pem, even before losing his cross, is in big trouble - with his faith, his church, his love life, and his bishop. These are his sermon notes, after a hospital visit:

"Open with that scene in the hospital, those good and righteous folk praying at the bedside of their minister. The humility of those people, their faith glowing like light around them, put me in such longing…to share their trustfulness.

"But then I asked myself: Must faith be blind? Why must it come of people's *need* to believe? We are all of us so pitiful in our desire to be unburdened, we will embrace Christianity or any other claim of God's authority for that matter. Look around. God's authority reduces us all, wherever we are in the world, whatever our tradition, to beggarly submission.

"So where is the truth to be found? Ecumenism is politically correct, *but what is the case?* If faith is valid in all its forms, are we merely making an aesthetic choice when we choose Jesus? And if you say, No, of course not, then we must ask, Who are the elect blessedly walking the true path to salvation…and who are the misguided others?… How do we distinguish our truth from another's falsity, we of the true faith, except by the story we cherish? Our story of God.

"But, my friends, I ask you: Is God a story? Can we, each of us examining our faith - I mean its pure center, not its consolations, not its habits, not its ritual sacraments - can we believe anymore in the heart of our faith that God is our story of Him? To presume to contain God in this Christian story of ours, to hold Him, circumscribe Him, the author of everything we can conceive and everything we cannot conceive… in *our* story of *Him? Of Her? OF WHOM?* What in the name of Christ do we think we are talking about?"

So he's hauled before his bishop. "Now listen, Pem. This is unseemly. You are doing and saying things that are…worrying. We're absolutely at a loss to know what is going on inside you. But I'm pretty sure you are not availing yourself of the strength to hand". To which Pem wishes he'd replied, "That may well be, but at least I don't do seances".

But back to that missing cross. He calls on the rabbis, and in the course of their discussions about who performed the act of desecration, and why, finds that they too are in spiritual crisis, rethinking and re-evaluating their own tradition. The God of the Jews is as dead as the God of the Christians, but he won't lie down for either of them.

Critically, Pem discovers that "Evolutionary Judaism" has more successfully come to terms with postmodernity than his own tradition, and he finds himself following the cross in its mysterious migration from church to synagogue. Evolutionary Judaism – derived in part from Mordecai Kaplan's Reconstruction Judaism and the more explicitly secular Humanistic Judaism synagogues – sounds very like a Jewish/American Sea of Faith Network, theologically and philosophically far more radical than the US Center for Progressive Christianity or the Jesus Seminar.

So the narrative core of the novel is the story of Father Pem's rediscovery and remaking of the "City of God", in the company, and later in the arms, of Rabbi Sarah Blumenthal (her husband and fellow rabbi being conveniently killed off to make room for a love which is as erotic as it is ecumenical). But around this soft core spins the hard maelstrom of intellectual ideas, cosmological and scientific, philosophical and political, which have first weakened and finally broken Pem's pre-postmodern faith. These are introduced by a somewhat bewildering assortment of bit-part players in the drama, who in turn take over the narration, in approved postmodern style: a journalist who is investigating the missing cross story, a movie-maker, a poet, a crooner. And as if that wasn't complicated enough, we also have pastiche-Wittgenstein, pastiche-Einstein, pastiche-Eliot, and pastiche-others-I-can't-identify. The reader has to work at *City of God* – a novel which takes it for granted that you'll bring a well-stocked mind to its pages.

And over it all hangs the shadow of the holocaust, told from Sarah's family history: the defining event of the twentieth century so far as a God accountable to humanity is concerned.

If the novel begins with the angst-ridden sermon which gets Father Pemberton the Anthony Freeman treatment, it ends with Rabbi Sarah's address to the "Conference of American Studies in Religion". Here's a long but edited extract:

"In the twentieth century about to end, the great civilizer on earth seems to have been doubt. Doubt, the constantly debated and flexible inner condition of theological uncertainty, the wish to believe in balance with rueful or nervous or grieving skepticism, seems to have held people in thrall to ethical behavior, while the true-believers, of whatever stamp, religious or religious-statist, have done the murdering. The impulse to excommunicate, to satanize, to eradicate, to ethnically cleanse, is a religious impulse. In the practice and politics of religion, God has always been a license to kill.

"But to hold in abeyance and irresolution any firm convictions of God, or of an afterlife with Him, warrants walking in His spirit, somehow. And among the doctrinaire religious, I find I trust those who gravitate towards symbolic comfort rather than those who reaffirm historic guarantees. It is just those uneasy promulgators of traditional established religion who are not in lockstep with its customs and practices, or who are chafing under doctrinaire pronouncements, or losing their congregations to charismatics and stadium-filling conversion performers, who are the professional religious I trust. The faithful who read Scripture in the way Coleridge defined the act of reading poetry or fiction, i.e., with a 'willing suspension of disbelief'.

"Yet they must be true to themselves and understand theirs is a compromised faith. Something more is required of them. Something more...

"I ask the question: Is it possible that the behavioral commandments of religion, its precipitate ethics or positive social values, can be maintained without reference to the authority of God?... I ask if after the exclusionary, the sacramental, the ritualistic, and simply fantastic elements of religion are abandoned, can a universalistic ethic be maintained - *in its numinousness?*...

"Suppose then that in the context of a hallowed secularism, the idea of God could be recognized as Something Evolving, as civilization has evolved - that God can be redefined, and recast, as the human race trains itself to a greater degree of metaphysical and scientific sophistication. With the understanding, in other words, that human history does show a pattern at least of progressively sophisticated metaphors...

"In this view, the supreme authority is not God, who is sacramentalized, prayed to, pleaded with, portrayed, textualized, or given voice, choir, or temple walls, but God who is imperceptible, ineffable, except for our evolved moral sense of ourselves...

"Dare we hope the theologians might emancipate themselves, so as to articulate or perceive another possibility for us in our quest for the sacred? Not just a new chapter, but a new story?

"There may not be much time. If the demographers are right, ten billion people will inhabit the earth by the middle of the coming century. Huge megacities of people all over the planet fighting for its resources. And perhaps with only the time-tested politics of God on their side to see them through. Under those circumstances, the prayers of mankind will sound to heaven as shrieks. And such abuses, shocks, to our hope for what life can be, as to make the twentieth century a paradise lost..."

Enough. Enough for you to judge whether I'm over-the-top when I say, if you read no other novel this year, read this one. And pray this prayer of ex-Father Tom Pemberton: "I think we must remake You. If we are to remake ourselves, we must remake You, Lord. We need a place to stand..."

Fiction, Theology, and the Critical Postmodernist

This essay is taken from two reviews, one of 'The Road to Reason' by Pat Duffy Hutcheon (Canadian Humanist Publications) £10, published in New Humanist, Summer 2001, and the other of 'Theology in the Fiction of George Eliot' by Peter C Hodgson (SCM Press) £17.95, published in SOF magazine, January 2002

Some of us in the Sea of faith Network, and even some of us who belong to or are attenders in that older S of F, the Society of Friends, call ourselves humanists, with or without a qualifying adjective ("religious", "Christian", "postmodern") and some of us flee from the word as from the wrath to come. But whether or not we see the SoF objective - promoting religious faith as a human creation - as a form of humanism, both these very different books help us understand the historical context within which radical secular theology developed.

Hutcheon's consists of 19 essays, mostly first published in the journal *Humanist in Canada*. Hutcheon identifies humanism with "evolutionary naturalism", and charts a linear progression from the Buddha to Richard Dawkins. The Buddha got the march to reason going by adroitly bypassing the gods and focusing on the human condition. The Greeks - Lucretius and Epicurus - took leave of gods and spirits altogether. Enlightenment thinkers like Hume privileged critical thinking based on reason and science, Darwin replaced the concept of creation by natural selection, and Dawkins gives the "road to reason" its ultimate destination. Humans are evolutionary creatures, and humanism itself has evolved from the proto-humanism of the Buddha to the "true humanism" of today's "evolutionary naturalism".

Well, up to a point, Lord Copper. This seems a pretty dated way of looking at things, rooted in a 19th century idea of progress which now seems quaint and inadequate. Having mapped out the road, our guide points out the "landmarks in the evolution of humanist thought" which lie on her strait and narrow line. But because this is the only road on Hutcheon's map, many towering landmarks are bypassed altogether. No place, then, for Chaucer or Shakespeare, for Winstanley or Blake, Shelley or Byron, Beethoven or Tippett. You'll need another map if you want to explore the scenic route which takes in Christian humanists like David Strauss and Ludwig Feuerbach, socialist humanists like William Morris and E P Thompson, religious humanists like George Eliot, or postmodern religious humanists like Don Cupitt.

Nevertheless, the book is a good read because Hutcheon writes very attractively and passionately about the landmark-humanists who fit her notion of progress towards reason. Particularly fine are the essays on the ethical humanism of Albert Schweitzer, Renaissance humanism and its Unitarian offshoots, and her celebration of Carl Sagan's devastating onslaughts on the new irrationality as it is expressed in endless varieties of gaseous spirituality and pseudo-scientific excursions into the "paranormal". I'd particularly recommend the Sagan essay - and, better, Sagan himself - to those who still want to dabble in what W S Gilbert called (in *Patience*) "only idle chatter of a transcendental kind".

Despite the primary focus on reason, however, Hutcheon does not underrate imagination, and it is here that she comes closest to the kind of broad, creative humanism which many of us would lay claim to. "Humanists", she writes, "believe the human species has evolved an imagination allowing us to envision possibilities not immediately available in past or current experience. They identify this imagination as the origin of all the gods that have been created in our image throughout history and pre-history. And they value it as the source of our architecture, music, literature and the visual arts". And, we might say, as the source of that amazing, crazy, inspirational and deadly-dangerous heritage of story, myth, poetry and ritual which we call religion.

George Eliot's name does not appear on Hutcheon's road map, no doubt because the great novelist's "religion of humanity" would look from Hutcheon's perspective to have too much warm religion about it and not enough cool reason. But Peter Hodgson's study, which deserves to be much more widely read and discussed than it is likely to be at the steep price of £17.95 for a rather drab-looking paperback, links Eliot's nineteenth century "theology" to the kinds of postmodern religious-humanist enquiry which Sea of Faith has been splashing about in for the last fifteen years. As a study of Eliot it is original and compelling. There is far more religion in Eliot's work than those who claim her for humanism normally allow, says Hodgson, and it's her take on religion which fits into a particular *critical* or *revisionist* postmodern theology.

An opening chapter takes us through the early biography of Mary Ann Evans, as she was called before she invaded (and conquered) a man's world with a man's name. Her evangelical childhood, when she rejected novels and fiction as lies, and therefore sinful; her rebellion and refusal to attend church; her involvement with the Coventry radicals (the best thing to have come out of the midlands city since Lady Godiva) whose critical approach to Bible scholarship and traditional theology led to her translating from German the two most influential theological books of the nineteenth century - Strauss's *Life of Jesus* and Feuerbach's *Essence of Christianity*. And so to the stream of magnificent novels including *Adam Bede*, *The Mill on the Floss*, *Middlemarch* and *Daniel Deronda*: a body of fiction with which only that of Dickens is remotely comparable in that century.

"Above all," comments Hodgson, "George Eliot was impressed by life's complexity and the ultimate mystery of things. She resisted simplistic solutions, whether on the side of supernaturalistic theism, materialistic atheism, scientific reductionism, or political utopianism." She was acutely conscious of religion's role as an opium of the people. She hated its "false shelter from present realities", its false promises, the false consolations of forms and ceremonies.

"The highest calling and election", she wrote, "is to *do without opium* and live through all our pain with conscious, clear-eyed endurance". She was (in Hodgson's words) "reluctant to engage in God-talk, knowing how readily such talk comes to the lips of humans, and how often it serves vain and petty interests". She looked for "a future religion without God-talk". Hodgson will not allow that she was an "atheist" (few theists will ever acknowledge their heroes and heroines as atheists), though he recognises that God never appears as an "empirical object or a direct agent" in her fiction. But the decisive transformations of the novels "are recounted in terms that suggest religious conversion, a process of death and rebirth, of losing and finding oneself, of creating a new kind of communal ethos defined by love and justice, which in the language of the Bible is something like the kingdom of God".

Eliot's novels *are* a kind of theology: or, more precisely, "theology itself is a kind of fiction that creates imaginative variations on what history offers as real in order to bespeak the mystery beneath the real". This kind of fiction/theology "approaches this mystery in terms of how redemptive transformations come about in ordinary life...Theology and art are both 'fiction' - a term deriving from the Latin verb *fingere*, 'to form', 'imagine', or 'invent' - in the sense that they entail a shaping, construing, configuring of the real in imaginative as opposed to empirical-descriptive modalities. They 'make things up', but they do so for purposes of illuminating reality, not escaping from it into a fantasy world". That's a powerful insight.

Eliot's fictional worlds, then, "envision something more than she herself was ever able to affirm directly. In the praxis of writing fiction she was able to overcome personal doubt and intellectual scepticism, and to enter a world of transformative possibilities". It is this distance between text and author, where "the world of the text may *explode* the world of the author", which brings Eliot close to "a certain kind of postmodern sensibility": not the extreme postmodern agnosticism which displaces any conviction with "don't know, can't know" and ends by burrowing up its own backside, but a "late modern" or "critical" or "revisionist" postmodernism which affirms fluidity, plurality, interrelatedness, the decentering of Western culture, and "wants to carry the unfinished project of modernity forward (with its focus on human rights, freedom, subjectivity, critical judgment) but in a vastly changed cultural world." Another brilliant insight.

Hodgson sums up his thesis: "I believe this is the kind of postmodernity that George Eliot most closely approximated. She was looking for ways through and beyond the aporias of modern culture (its secularism, Philistinism, cynicism, dehumanization) but without abandoning its gains and without returning to the past with its repressive orthodoxies. She did this by attempting to envision new possibilities, a religion for the future, a more perfect religion... Her question was: what is the lasting meaning that lies in all religious doctrine?... We have to assume that the 'more perfect religion' and the 'lasting meaning' will appear not in a single universal religion but in a diversity of concrete religious faiths and practices."

Most of Pat Duffy Hutcheon's landmark humanists on the "road to reason" have contributed something to modern religious humanism, but none have contributed more than the creator of Dorothea, Dinah, Maggie, Hetty, Adam, Felix and Daniel. Peter Hodgson is a brilliant and stimulating interpreter of her fictive theology. But read the novels to discover afresh what happens when a religious sensibility discovers the joys of secular intercourse.

Passion Play

'It seems that there are still new, new ways of telling the old, old story...' This review of Covent Garden's brave and imaginative production of Bohuslav Martinu's lyrical opera 'The Greek Passion' was published in SOF magazine, July 2000

It must be millennium fever at work, but it's remarkable how much so-called "high culture" this year has been explicitly religious in tone and content. We've noted in recent *SOF* issues the big gallery events: *Seeing Salvation* at the National, *Heaven* at the Liverpool Tate, *Taste - the New Religion* in Manchester. This year's BBC Proms season is about "faith in the future" and concentrates on "music inspired by man's relationship with God". Even Harrison Birtwistle has turned in a postmodern opera-oratorio about the Last Supper.

And in May the newly-refurbished Royal Opera House at Covent Garden bravely revived Martinu's extraordinary opera *The Greek Passion*, which is about Christ's passion and human passion: a play on passion, based on a passion play.

The opera is derived from the novel *Christ Recrucified* by the Greek communist writer Nikos Kazantzakis (whose work also inspired Martin Scorsese's film *The Last Temptation of Christ*). It is set in a Greek/Turkish village in the 1920s, during the appalling atrocities by which one and a half million Greeks were driven out of their homes in a bloody population exchange which set the scene for later waves of ethnic cleansing. This is no nymphs-and-shepherds fantasy. The passions to be explored are those of our own familiar world.

It is Easter and acting-parts are being allocated for the village passion play. The popular postman will play Peter, the unpopular tanner Judas. Katerina, the village girl who is no better than she should be (an expression I have never understood), is naturally typecast as Mary Magdalen. A farm labourer, Manolios, gets the plum part of Jesus. They rehearse the text - and start asking each other what these oddly baffling words - "Blessed are the poor in spirit... the meek... those who love their enemies" - can possibly mean. Where could the script-writer have found such disturbing lines, defying all notions of common sense?

Gradually the actors become engrossed in their parts, and begin to be transformed by the words they are learning. Manolios loses all interest in his promised marriage to Lenio, the ardent young illegitimate daughter of the richest man in the village. But he doesn't lose interest in sex. He has passionate dreams of Katerina, and she of him. He is playing God made flesh, and Katerina is flesh made divine.

As they wonder how to square their passion for each other with the demands of the passion play, into the village bursts a flood of asylum seekers, fleeing from the latest bout of ethnic cleansing. They are hungry, sick, frightened. What is to be done with them? Build detention centres? Give them food vouchers? Grigoris, the village-priest-cum-Home-Secretary, has no doubts. They will take our jobs and give us their diseases. And most of them are probably *bogus*. They must be turned away.

Our passion players are not so sure. How would this fit with all that oddly haunting stuff about mercy, pity, love? They encourage the refugees to stay, finding some food for them and facing the hostility of the forces of conservatism among their neighbours. Manolios and Katerina subordinate their physical passion for each other to their passionate concern for their new neighbours. Meanwhile, Lenio has understandably given up on her promised spouse and found another lover, a young shepherd named Nikolio, and, oblivious to the political crisis engulfing the village, they make their own delightful passion play, under the open skies.

The village elders and Grigoris are furious because of the unsettling effect the now Christ-like Monolios is having on the village. He is excommunicated from the very church where he is about to play Jesus. Angry and bitter at their hostile treatment by Grigoris and his followers, the asylum-seekers start talking of seizing land and food by violence. Manolios continues to take their part: how can anyone mouth texts about blessing the poor whilst driving the poor away? Grigoris stirs up the crowd, and in a horrifying climax the tanner-Judas strangles Manolios-Jesus at the foot of his cross.

The end? Not quite. A resurrection, then? Too obvious! This is the real world! The band of passion players is scattered. Up in the mountains, the refugees survive a summer and prepare for a cold winter, knowing that Manolios has been sacrificed on their behalf, and that his death has done nothing to improve their lot or soften the hearts of their oppressors:

salvation has been postponed, for reasons beyond anyone's control.

Down in the village, normality restored by the dispersal of the asylum-seekers, the priest Grigoris leads his flock in preparations for Christmas. For both communities, the great religious festivals at the heart of their communal life go on, either as consolation in defeat or as celebration of victory. True religion and undefiled is neither the "Christos anesti!" of a Greek Easter nor the "Happy Christmas!" of a western winter solstice. So what is it?

Well, what about young Lenio and Nikolio? They alone extricate themselves from the politics and the religion, to make love, not war. Theirs is not the passion of the cross but the passion of human flesh and blood. They have better uses for their lips than preaching, better ways to spend an Easter or a Christmas than singing hymns...

Martinu would seem to be saying that religion hasn't been much of a success in saving either the wretched or the self-righteous. As the opera ends, the asylum seekers are still seeking asylum, the villagers intone their intoxicating liturgies, apparently oblivious of the demands made on them by the words they sing, Manolios is dead and his comrades scattered. Only Lenio and Nikolio, who couldn't give a damn for religion or politics, have found happiness in each other. All you need is love?

It is still not that simple. I suspect that what we learn from the denoument of the passion play itself - that what happens to Monolios is what has happened to saviours before him, and will happen to saviours to come - applies no less to the lovers who so nimbly separate themselves from the main action. So as we wonder what will become of the betrayed refugees, of Katerina and her fellow-players, of the murderer Judas, and of the smug Hallelujah-singers in Grigoris's church, we also wonder how long Lenio and Nikolio will make love under the Greek sun. Do we suppose that the intensity of their feelings for each other can be sustained indefinitely? By both of them? Or is their passion play in the wings as transient, and as apparantly pointless, as the one that occupies centre stage?

This is a profoundly ambiguous opera. There is nothing black and white about it. Its ambiguity was probably one of the reasons it was at first rejected by Covent Garden in 1957 when it was considered "unlikely to appeal to the exclusive, intellectual audience" the culture-snobs who ran the place wanted to attract. Martinu actually wrote a second version, less ambiguous, better calculated to appeal to an audience looking for a more conventional treatment of the theme. Thankfully, director David Pountney, conductor Charles Mackerras and the current Covent Garden management had the courage to go for the complex original rather than the sanitised revision.

"The two great themes", wrote Martinu, "are like thin trickles of blood: the heritage of man's Christian virtues and his obligations to humanity". *The Greek Passion* is a truly magnificent reworking of "the greatest story ever told". Unhappily, the Royal Opera gave it only six performances - so if you missed it, you missed it. Watch out for a revival.

One for the Dark Lord:
on Faith and Fantasy

These reflections on the book and film 'The Lord of the Rings' were written for SOF magazine, March 2002

I am not the most detached, objective commentator when it comes to writing about *The Lord of the Rings*. I was introduced to the world of Tolkein's Middle Earth in the fifties when I noticed that my Crusader bible-class leader was talking less about Jesus and more about Frodo Baggins, Gandalf, Gollum and the Balrog. Intrigued, I soon made myself the proud owner of the first-edition set of three hardbacks - the ones with those magical black and red maps on folded rice-paper at the back. I was hooked on enchantment.

When I got married, we made the *Ring* trilogy our first book at bedtime. It took a year to get through, during which we shared our bed with Aragorn and Arwen, or, on bad nights, with Shelob. Seven or eight years later I was reading it again, this time to our two daughters, reassuring them every night that daddy would see to orcs, Black Riders, or Sauron himself if they appeared when the light was switched off. I came back to it when the BBC's 26-part radio serial hit the air in the eighties, and now it's our book at bedtime again. So you might say I'm lost to the Dark Lord on his dark throne, in the land of Mordor where the shadows lie.

It was therefore with some apprehension that I went to see the first of the three films, *The Fellowship of the Ring*. Tolkein's imaginary world had long been worked over by *my* imagination, but now my imagination was to be worked over by Peter Jackson's. Could his Black Riders match mine? Could his Rivendell be the heaven, his Mordor the hell, that Tolkien's text and maps and runes had made them for me over forty years? Was it possible that Gandalf, hobbits, dwarves, elves and the dreaded Nazgul, hitherto all in the mind, could survive an incarnation in flesh - prosthetic ears, beards, hairy feet, special effects and all? Could Bilbo still be Bilbo with Ian Holm's head on his shoulders, or Gandalf Gandalf when he speaks with Ian McEllen's familiar voice? How could *any* mortal man play Frodo the Halfling?

The short answer is that Jackson succeeds brilliantly. Indeed, it has to be admitted that the film version actually improves on the book in some respects, such as its wise omission of virtually all the fey and folksy songs which Tolkein himself should have junked as somewhat wearisome and whimsical interruptions of his epic narrative. And the New Zealand settings are magical - as the NZ tourist industry has already noticed.

Only if you live neither on Middle Earth nor Planet Earth will you be ignorant of the story: the Dark Lord Sauron seeks the one ring that will enable him to spread his evil power over the whole world; the ring is lost, but Bilbo finds it and entrusts it to the keeping of his nephew Frodo; only if the ring can be thrown into the Crack of Doom, guarded by Sauron's apparatus of evil, can its power be broken and the evil be conquered; and with his tiny fellowship of hobbits and friends, led by the wizard Gandalf, Frodo makes the epic journey against impossible odds to save the world from death and destruction.

The story has of course been interpreted as allegory, with the ring itself being seen as the symbol of every conceivable manifestation of evil, from the threat of Nazism to the march of modernity - which Tolkein, as a conservative Catholic, feared and loathed. In the late fifties my generation tended to link the ring with our own contemporary symbol of evil: nuclear weapons. We marched to Aldermaston as to Mordor, and when we sang

"Don't you hear the H-bomb's thunder
Echo like the crack of doom...?"

we merged two potent mythologies.

But Tolkein was insistent that his work was not an allegory, and particularly not an allegorical gloss on the Christian version of Good versus Evil. He acknowledged that Gandalf, who lays down his life for his friends, descends into the bottomless pit of Moria, then rises again, transfigured, has certain similarities to Christ, and he was prepared to defend his creation as not inconsistent with Catholicism. But, he insisted, "I have not put in, or have cut out, practically all references to anything like 'religion'...The religious element is absorbed into the story". He was content to leave moralistic preachy stuff to his friend CS Lewis, with his evangelical Narnia stories and the awful *Perelandra*. The *Ring* trilogy - itself no more than an episode in history of Middle Earth, told more fully in *The Silmarillion* - was an epic story, no more, no less. It was fantasy on a scale to rival that of Homer.

Those who can't abide the *Ring* usually ascribe their distaste to one of two reasons. The first simply finds the story reactionary, if not racist and sexist to boot. The goodies are all white (whether hobbit, elf, dwarf, wizard or man), the baddies all black (the Nazgul, the orcs, even Sauron's swans). Females are rarely either seen or heard. When they are, their role is to look radiant, to sing some of Tolkein's soppiest songs, and stand by their elf (or whatever). It is impossible to imagine any of them having sex (though that is equally true of the males). How hobbits get made is a mystery.

These objections seem to me trivial: rather like criticising *Beowulf* for having too much violence, or Shakespeare's *Merchant of Venice* for picking on Jews. Or, for that matter, tut-tutting over the Bible for its racist assumption of one tribe as God's chosen people, and one half of humanity as derived from the spare rib of the other. Certainly, all these things are offensive. But please God it will never be the function of art to be politically/morally correct. Would we have Don Giovanni a chaste monk, or require that Carmen keep her legs crossed?

The other objection is that the *Ring* is fantasy - and fantasy is whimsical, childish, escapist. Fantasy is untrue! There *are* no hobbits, so why all this pretend-stuff? To my surprise, Don Cupitt seemed to endorse this view in a recent *Guardian* "Face to Faith" column, when he dismissed the works of Tolkein, Lewis and Philip Pullman as "crazy" because they "invoke all the old supernatural apparatus" and fail to appreciate that the old sacred and pre-scientific universe is a thing of the past. Fantasy, he argued, belongs to childhood, and when we become adults we must put away childish things. Our affection for fantasy is no more than an expression of nostalgia for the supernatural, which our heads left behind when we grew up, but our hearts obstinately cling to. "We need to make a clean break with [fantasy] for our own good".

What is surprising is that this view of fantasy, of story, seems to contradict everything Don has been telling us over the past few years. We live by stories. We make sense of life through stories. Our values are embodied in stories, narratives and meta-narratives. The *Gilgamesh* epics, the *Odyssey*, the Hindu *Mahabharata*, the Old Testament story of the making of a people and the New Testament one of the word made flesh, *Beowulf*, *Canterbury Tales*, Shakespeare's Puck and Prospero, Blake's complex mythology, *Alice in Wonderland*, *Star Trek* ... These are our stories, these are our songs.

What is fantasy if not imagination in flight? And what does it mean to be human if not to imagine, to fantasise? Fantasy is art, and art is what makes us only a little lower than the angels (themselves a splendid product of human fantasy!). My *Shorter English Dictionary on Historical Principles* gives a range of definitions of fantasy and they fall into two types, narrow and broad. The narrow definitions emphasise illusion, caprice, whim, but the broader ones emphasise "imagination... the process, the faculty or the result of forming representations of things not actually present".

Ah, I hear, but *Lord of the Rings* is only second-hand fantasy, a *contrived* epic, cobbled together from Norse sagas, Anglo-Saxon chronicles, Celtic dreams, and Wagnerian rehashes of all the above. Who is the Balrog if not *Beowulf's* Grendel, who Gandalf if not the archetypal saviour, who Frodo if not a miniature Siegfried with hairy toes? But of course Tolkein's epic is "contrived"! So too is every epic, every story, every work of art and imagination. A committee calling itself Moses contrived the Pentateuch and the Ten Commandments, another called David contrived the Psalms. *Contriving* is what it's all about! "Contrive: to make, create, imagine; to devise with ingenuity and cleverness; to bring to pass".

Fantasy, imagination, make-believe, poetry: they are of one family. And if theology too is a poetry, it is part of the same kith and kin. Fantasies like Tolkein's play with hobbits, orcs, elves and dwarves: the poetry we call theology plays with gods and angels, devils and demons. Both conjure up (contrive) imagined beings to play out human roles. Both provide a language by which we can say something about the human condition which cannot easily or adequately be said in plain everyday speech.

Fantasy and theology are both fictions. "Theology itself is a kind of fiction that creates imaginative variations on what history offers as real in order to bespeak the mystery beneath the real". So writes Peter Hodgson in *Theology in the Fiction of George Eliot*. The mystery beneath the real is approached by fictive theology "in terms of how redemptive transformations come about in ordinary life". He pushes the point home by reminding us that *fiction* derives from the Latin verb "fingere", to form, imagine or invent. It is in this vital sense that theology, art, fantasy are one: In Hodgson's words, they all "entail a shaping, construing, configuring of the real in imaginative as opposed to empirical-descriptive modalities. They 'make things up', but they do so for purposes of illuminating reality, not escaping from it".

Which is why it is so hard to see why Don Cupitt commends the stories of theology (provided we understand them as fictions) but warns us against the stories of fantasy (equally understood as belonging to the realm of the imagination). Such selectivity would seem to leave us with a somewhat impoverished mindscape: gods but no goblins, holy ghosts but no ringwraiths, angels but no hobbits - and the fancies of religious fiction but not those of Homer, Shakespeare Asimov or Tolkein.

The logic of Don's position is that we should make a "clean break" not only with those fantasy-fictions which deal with human creations like hobbits, orcs, wizards and things that go bump in the night, but also with those older fantasy-fictions which deal with human creations like gods, spirits, devils and demons. I prefer his earlier view: that, *provided we clearly understand that our fantasies ARE fictions, that the supernatural is itself a human fancy*, the old, old stories still have much to tell us about ourselves and the world we inhabit.

No-one reading the *Ring* books or seeing the film supposes their supernaturalist framework is anything but a fiction. Those of us who understand the supernaturalist framework of religion and all its stories to be another form of   fiction are not being nostalgic for a lost past, but imaginative in our appropriation of a rich heritage of story-telling.

It would be absurdly simplistic to boil down a work of such epic proportions, and of such richness, to a one-paragraph sound-byte. But if I were to attempt a summary of what *The Lord of the Rings* says to me, it would be something like this:

I would begin by noting that there is no objective God in Middle Earth (or even above it). No Lord of Light to match the Dark Lord. Sauron is the *only* lord, and he is the evil one. This is a most unusual fantasy world where there is a Lucifer but no Jehovah. The ring is Sauron's magic instrument, and there is no countervailing instrument for good. The fellowship cannot therefore call to the heavens for salvation, for they are empty. Frodo and his little band stand alone, pitting only their weakness, innocence, common sense, decency (and the odd bit of fancy magic) against the mighty armies and monsters of Mordor. Despite his death, resurrection and second coming, Gandalf is no God. And it is the very weakness and innocence of Frodo which marks him out as far less likely than the clever Gandalf, the wise Elrond, the aristocratic Aragorn or the mighty Boromir to succumb to the temptation to wield the all-corrupting ring for his own purposes.

What has to be done to overcome evil (the lust for absolute power which the ring signifies) has to be done by mere mortals, led by an innocent who has no ambition for himself, and who does it because he must, not out of obedience to anyone or Anyone. Not by raising a mighty army to match the Dark Lord's swarming orcs, nor by yielding to the deadly temptation of using Sauron's ring against him, but by fellowship, courage, simplicity, integrity. The fellowship knows it is on its own: no saviour from on high delivers. Tolkein claimed to have cut religion out of the trilogy, and he certainly leaves out God. But the human spirit - God in every man, hobbit, elf and dwarf - is the final victor at the Crack of Doom.

The Ten Suggestions

The following article was written for The Guardian, but not published. It proposed ten hypothetical propositions, previously published for discussion and debate in SOF magazine

Ten is a good round number. By giving us ten fingers God made a decimal point. The Church of England surely overplayed its hand when it went for no fewer than 39 Articles. Moses knew what he was doing when he came down from the mountain with one commandment for each digit: this finger for murder, that one for adultery, and a thumb's down for coveting your neighbour's ass.

But we are no longer comfortable with commandments, particularly when they are written on a stone tablet so that you can't change a word unless you've learnt how to use a hammer and chisel. I'd prefer Ten Suggestions - or, as the Quakers say, "Advices", though they have a lot more than Moses' ten and the C of E's 39. Let's call them "hypotheses".

"Hypothesis" is defined by the Shorter OED as "a proposition or principle put forth or stated merely as a basis for reasoning and argument... a provisional supposition which serves as a starting-point for further investigation". Hypotheses are *not* credal articles of faith, let alone commandments. They are there to encourage argument, discussion, investigation and clarification. The set of hypotheses I'm proposing here takes as its starting point the modern view that religion in all its forms is a wholly human creation - an overarching hypothesis in its own right - and aims to *try out* a number of ways of expressing this view which contrive to be true both to the best of our religious heritage and to a mature, reasonable twenty-first century outlook.

They have already been picked up for discussion in churches, Quaker groups and modern religious networks in Britain, Australia, New Zealand, California and Canada. But if any organisation were to adopt them as a Creed, it would spectacularly miss the point.

Tick them all and you fail the test! If some, at least, don't stimulate you to snorts of rage or derision, they are just not doing the business. Affirm where you can, amend where you can't. If you don't want to be a do-it-yourself thinker, go back to the Ten Commandments.

1. No set of statements about religious faith will ever tell the truth, the whole truth and nothing but the truth. This naturally holds good for the hypotheses that follow.

2. All religions, faith systems and varieties of religious or spiritual faith and practice are human constructs: part of the wondrous complex of experience, imagination, accumulated knowledge, creativity and reflective consciousness which we call culture. We may speak of the divine, the transcendent and the ultimate, but we do so in the understanding that these are human concepts. Human communities created them. Human communities made it all up.

3. We live a natural life in a natural world, which is made intelligible to us through the signs and symbols of language. We may speak of the supernatural, but we do so in the understanding that this too is a human concept, the product of human imagination, story-telling and myth-making.

4. As religion is the product of the creative impulse, so too are its gods and godesses, angels and devils. They are human creations, made by human communities, reflecting our rich variety of histories, languages and cultures. "All deities reside in the human breast" (Blake). This is no less true of the god of the great monotheist traditions, the god named God. The Creator God is our creation, the Father God our projection, the Saviour God our own solution to our own inadequacies and alienation. Heaven is the best we can imagine, hell the worst, and both are here and now.

5. Sacred scriptures, stories and songs have provided sense, meaning and purpose, have helped us see visions and dream dreams; but they are fallible and subject to criticism and reinterpretation. To belittle them impoverishes our heritage, but to elevate them into expressions of eternal truth is dangerous.

6. Our faith is "religious" in the depth of its seriousness and the sincerity of its commitment: but it is also "secular" in the literal sense of its being of this world and for this age. In a world where the supernatural is natural and the divine is human, the sacred and the secular are one. As we secularize our faith, so we also sacralize our lives. That is our commitment.

7. We are believers. We choose to believe and have faith in the values of

"mercy, pity, peace and love", and things which are "true, honest, just, lovely and of good report". The worship of God, if that is what we choose to call it, as an inspiration and symbol, affirms these values as expressions of the wholly human spirit.

8. True religion is incomplete and delusory unless it is concerned with injustice and suffering, particularly among the powerless and hungry. False religion invokes a crude supernaturalism to validate authority, sanctify power, provoke fear and superstition, foster division and gull the gullible. It offers heaven as compensation for earthly woes or reward for obedience, and threatens hell for disobedience, making God a tyrant, and religion itself the instrument of tyranny.

9. The life of faith is a life of change, growth, renewal: a life of exploration and experimentation, of making new discoveries and discarding them when they fail us. It is a life on the ocean wave, not one that seeks the seclusion of a safe harbour. It is for the seeker, not the finder; for those who would make meaning and purpose rather than buy them off the peg. It demands hope, charity, determination - and a sense of humour.

10. We should lay no claim to eternal truth. But we should cherish the best in our heritage of faith, tradition and practice as we cherish the best in our heritage of music, poetry, the arts, the sciences, and everything that gives imaginative expression to the wholly human spirit. We made it, and because we made it we can refashion it to meet our changing needs, understandings and experience. To explore and promote religious faith as a human creation, a human recreation, a human responsibility, and as a source of delight to ourselves and an affirmation of our sense of responsibility for the welfare of our living world: this is our challenge and our adventure.

DAVID BOULTON is a member of the Quaker Universalist Group and an attender at Brigflatts Quaker meeting, Cumbria. He was editor of the Sea of Faith magazine SOF from 1992-2002 and Head of News, Current Affairs and Arts at Granada Television, 1980-90. He is currently a member of the Broadcasting Standards Commission. After his books on contemporaty issues were published by W H Allen, Cape and Macmillan, he started Dales Historical Monographs to publish work on local and Quaker history. He lives in Dent, Cumbria, with his wife Anthea.